WINTER NOTES
ON
SUMMER IMPRESSIONS

D0813864

WINTER NOTES
ON
SUMMER
IMPRESSIONS

Fyodor Dostoevsky

Fedor M Dostoevskii

Translated by
David Patterson

Northwestern University Press
Evanston, IL

ALBRIGHT COLLEGE LIBRARY

Northwestern University Press
Evanston, IL 60201

Printed in the United States of America

Translation and notes © 1988 David Patterson. All rights
reserved.

Winter Notes on Summer Impressions is a translation of
Zimnie zametki o letnikh vpechlatleniyakh in F. M.
Dostoevsky, *Polnoe sobranie sochinenii*, Volume 5 (Leningrad:
Gosudarstvo, 1973).

Library of Congress Cataloging-in-Publication Data

Dostoyevsky, Fyodor, 1821–1881.
    [Zimnie zametki o letnikh vpechatleniĩakh. English]
    Winter notes on summer impressions / Fyodor Dostoevsky;
translated by David Patterson.
      p.   cm.
    Translation of: Zimnie zametki o letnikh vpechatleniĩakh.
    ISBN 0-8101-0813-5. ISBN 0-8101-0814-3 (pbk.)
    1. Dostoyevsky, Fyodor, 1821–1881—Journeys—Europe. 2. Europe—
Description and travel—1800–1918. I. Patterson, David.
II. Title
PG3328.A1713 1988
891.78'303—dc19
[B]   88-28945
                                        CIP

891.753
D724w;

218296

8.95

CONTENTS

Introduction

On 7 June 1862 Fyodor Mikhailovich Dostoevsky (1821–81) left Petersburg on his first excursion to Europe, the "land of holy wonders," as he ironically termed it. Over the next ten weeks he visited several capitals and other cities, including Berlin, Wiesbaden, Dresden, Paris, London, Geneva, Florence, Vienna, and others. He recorded his impressions of Europe, particularly those of Paris and London, and published them as *Winter Notes on Summer Impressions* in the February 1863 issue of *Vremya (Time),* a periodical published by his brother Mikhail and edited by himself. His reason for making the journey to the West, as he explained it to his younger brother Andrey, was to consult some specialists about his epilepsy. But surely there was also the lure of the roulette tables, for Dostoevsky was a compulsive gambler; indeed, he lost a substantial sum during his stay in Wiesbaden, where he went after spending only a day in Berlin. Perhaps the most important reason of all, however, was to see firsthand the source of the ideas which, he believed, were corrupting Russia, ideas that produced such despairing and divided figures as the underground man in his *Notes from Underground* (1864) and Ivan Karamazov in *The Brothers Karamazov* (1880). Thus Dostoevsky did not take in the usual tourist sights but spent his time primarily on the streets of the European cities, observing people rather than things. *Winter Notes,* then, is a book about human beings and being human—penetrating, insightful, and critical.

Less than three years before his trip to Europe Dostoevsky returned from Siberia, where he had spent four years at hard labor and another six years in exile for his involvement in the radical Petrashevsky Circle. Drawing from his experience in prison, he set to work on the first major literary project to follow his exile; the result was *Notes from the House of the Dead* (1860–62), a novel that marks an important turning point in the development of his art as well as his ideas. In *Winter Notes* we find echoes of a major concern that runs throughout *House of the Dead:* the conflict between the one and the many, between the human being and the inhuman state, between the single individual and the encompassing society. This concern comes to light most explicitly in *Winter Notes* when Dostoevsky discusses the notion of brotherhood, particularly in Chapter Six. In his view, one of the biggest stumbling blocks to brotherhood is an egocentrism steeped in the formulas and slogans of monologism. Here freedom is translated into the multiplication, satisfaction, and justification of desires; life is lived in the dative case, as it were, ruled by the mentality and the language of "to me" and "for me." Entrenched in a self-centered monologue and haunted by fear, the individual neither seeks nor offers a responsive word but endeavors to have the last word.

Genuine brotherhood, on the other hand, lies in communal interaction and mutual renunciation of self-interest on the part of the individual and society. Here the freedom born of brotherhood lies in dialogical relation, in responsibility for and responsiveness to one another; grounded in a spontaneous love which is the opposite of fear and the basis of dialogue, it is constituted by a life lived from an attitude of "I for the sake of the other." The highest expression of freedom, love, and brotherhood—in short, the highest development of the human being—comes with the total sacrifice of the self for the other. We have only as much life as we give, only as much love as we offer. The point is that the love required for such a human community cannot be fabricated by formulas or dictated by authority; it is more a matter of dialogical relation than monological prescription, more a question of interaction than reaction.

As a text, indeed, *Winter Notes* is itself shaped by dialogical interaction running throughout its literary form and narrative voice. The dialogism in the work brings to mind the theories of Mikhail Bakhtin, although Bakhtin does not discuss *Winter Notes* in his *Problems of Dostoevsky's Poetics*. Nevertheless, in keeping with Bakhtin's thinking, we note that its thematic opposition to materialism and bourgeois culture is of a piece with its structural features, so that the literary experiment is a formal expression of the ideological response. Looking more closely at Dostoevsky's exploration of literary boundaries, we find that the narrator's voice is in fact a multitude of voices. Here we may observe the frequent insertion of parenthetical remarks, the recurring rendition of the narrator's inner dialogues, and the use of phrases and citations set off from the text by indentation or quotation marks. One gets the impression that *Winter Notes* is not simply a text but a text about the process of producing a text. The narrator's interaction with himself, moreover, parallels his interaction with the reader. He opens the text, for instance, by addressing his "friends," putting his questions to them and anticipating their rejoinders; then—as if the reader's stance were not complex enough—he makes a distinction between his "friends" and "the reader" at the end of Chapter Two. The position of the reader is complicated further still when the narrator states in Chapter One and repeats in Chapter Five that he may be lying but it is with the conviction that he is telling the truth. Thus as he responds to the monologism of the West, the narrator himself takes on a number of voices and viewpoints on a number of levels.

In the process of making his point, Dostoevsky introduces several other dialogical dimensions to his literary text. We find the voices of sundry other figures, for example, interacting with the narrator's voice. Dostoevsky's long paragraphs underscore the multitude of voices within the voice. Then there is the insertion of French words and phrases, the frequent use of ellipses and open-ended sentences, and the ongoing allusion to other authors whose very names conjure up a multitude of ideological voices. The constant sidetracking also points up the work's dialogical dimensions, since it establishes a tension between the title of a given chapter and its content. Perhaps the most obvious dialogical feature of the text is irony, which is always double-voiced. A glaring example of irony—and of the tension between a chapter's title and its content—is Chapter Three, titled "And a Superfluous One." Yet it is anything but superfluous, for it establishes the foundation underlying not only the investigation of Europe and the problem of Russianness but also the dialogical aspects of the work. The text's irony arrives at its culmination in Chapter Eight, where the narrator takes the terms *bribri* and *ma biche* out of their familiar setting and places them in an alien, that is, his own critical context; the very use of those appellations thus constitutes a cultural and ideological critique.

A primary target of that critique is the French bourgeois, whose life is squandered in the accumulation of money and the acquisition of things. Schooled in the European Enlightenment and the objective ways of reason, the bourgeois has reduced himself to an object. Instead of thinking of himself in terms of a living inner presence, he identifies himself with the dead things outside of himself, with what is pleasing to the eye. Instead of a life grounded in a loving and responsive relation to his fellow human beings, he founders in a living death geared to the buying and selling of himself and others. Instead of embracing a truth and thus making a life, he has turned himself over to the lie of making a living. To be sure, much of *Winter Notes* is devoted to unmasking this lie which passes for eloquence, this depravity which pretends to be virtue. Central to the project of exposing the lie is, again, the literary form of the text itself—its multitude of voices and dialogical interaction over against the monological "catechism on virtue" and the sloganism of *liberté, égalité, fraternité*. Yet despite the severity of this critique of the bourgeois, the Frenchman does not prove to be completely void of spirit, for Dostoevsky sees in the bourgeois a repressed anxiety, a quiet desperation, which is an essential dimension of the self as spirit and which underscores the human in human being.

While distinctly his own, Dostoevsky's treatment of the bourgeois in *Winter Notes* reflects the influence of the Russian exile Aleksandr Herzen (1812–70), particularly Herzen's *Letters from France and Italy* (1847–52), and *From the Other Shore* (1847–50). In these works Herzen takes his own critical look at the bourgeoisie and outlines his hopes for an ultimately victorious proletariat. Herzen rejected European civilization and believed it was incapable of the regeneration that was needed to restore a human life to what had become inhuman; and, like Dostoevsky, he looked to Russia for salvation. Herzen's influence on Dostoevsky, moreover, was not only ideological but formal as well, since Herzen's works, too, represent experiments in textual form, and explorations of literary boundaries. Dostoevsky, in fact, visited Herzen while he was in London; there Dostoevsky also met Mikhail Bakunin (1814–76), the exiled Russian anarchist and friend of Vissarion Belinsky (1811–48), the thinker and critic largely responsible for Dostoevsky's early fame as a writer.

The sights and sounds of the street life in London left perhaps an even greater impression on Dostoevsky than those in Paris, at least in terms of the details that showed up in his subsequent works. In *Notes from Underground,* for example— the work which immediately follows *Winter Notes*—the underground man's rejection of the Crystal Palace as a symbol of Western man's ultimate realization of truth reflects Dostoevsky's own attitude toward the new palace that housed the 1862 International Exhibition in London. Scenes from *The Gambler* (1866), furthermore, are reminiscent of Dostoevsky's description of a London casino and the striking young woman he saw there. Probably the most indelible impression that London left on Dostoevsky came from a ragged little girl whom he encountered on a street in the Haymarket. The look of fear and hunger that marked her face and the image of her bruised body never left him; it was as though the lost and suffering children of the world gazed at him through those despairing eyes. Perhaps she is the little girl who reappears fourteen years later in his "Dream of a Ridiculous Man" as the child who summons the love and thus effects the salvation of the ridiculous man.

The impressions which produced *Winter Notes,* however, had a greater impact on Dostoevsky's later writings than simply lending a detail here and there. Planted in this short work are the seeds of many of the collisions that distinguish the dialogue of ideas in his great novels. Examples include Raskolnikov's concept of the Napoleonic crime in *Crime and Punishment* (1866); Myshkin's implicit challenge to Western culture in his rejection of egotism and ambition in *The Idiot* (1868); the critique of revolutionary ruthlessness and conservative stupidity in *The Possessed* (1872); and, in *The Brothers Karamazov,* the theme that if a grain of wheat should fall to the earth and die, it will produce much fruit. The polyphony of voices in interaction with each other, which is a stylistic feature of *Winter Notes,* is also a distinguishing aspect of the subsequent major works; in those works Dostoevsky not only continues but refines the literary investigations of *Winter Notes.* Thus, while modest in its scope, *Winter Notes* contains considerable depth in its significance; indeed, it is essential to any serious study of Dostoevsky. On the surface it is a dialogue between what is Russian and what is European, as well as an innovation in literary form. But underneath there is the struggle between truth and lie, spirit and mammon, life and death.

What Dmitri Karamazov says of the mystery and the terror surrounding beauty may also be said of the undercurrents that stir in *Winter Notes:* God and the devil are fighting there, and the field of battle is the human heart.

1

In Place of a Foreword

For some months now, my friends, you have been urging me to hurry up and describe to you my impressions from abroad, never suspecting that your request simply has me at my wit's end. What shall I write for you? What can I say that is new, as yet unknown, that has not been said before? Who among all of us Russians (that is, those who at least read the journals) does not know Europe twice as well as he knows Russia? I put "twice" here out of courtesy, but ten times is more accurate. In addition, aside from these general considerations, you no doubt know that I have nothing in particular to relate and even less to properly write because I saw nothing properly myself, and what I did see I had no time to examine. I was in Berlin, Dresden, Wiesbaden, Baden-Baden, Cologne, Paris, London, Lucerne, Geneva, Genoa, Florence, Milan, Vienna—twice in some places—and I traveled to all these places, all of them, in exactly two and a half months! Tell me, is it really possible to examine anything properly when such a long journey has been made in two and a half months? You will recall that I drew up my itinerary beforehand, while still in Petersburg. I had never been abroad. I had longed to go almost since my earliest childhood, from the time when I spent long winter evenings, before I could read, listening open-mouthed, paralyzed with ecstasy and terror, as my parents read to me the novels of Radcliffe[1] at bedtime; then I would rave deliriously about them in my

1

sleep. Finally, at the age of forty, I broke loose and went abroad; needless to say, I wanted to see not only as much as possible but everything, absolutely everything, despite the limited time. Moreover, I was certainly in no condition to calmly select the places to visit. Lord, I expected so much from this trip! "Even if I don't study anything in detail," I thought, "I'll still have seen everything and been everywhere; I'll still form a whole picture from everything I see, a kind of overall panorama. The entire 'land of holy wonders'[2] will unfold before me all at once, from a bird's-eye view, like the Promised Land viewed from the perspective of a mountain top. In a word, I shall receive some new, wondrous, powerful impression." And now what is it that saddens me most, as I sit at home and recall my summer wanderings? Not the fact that I did not examine anything in detail but that I went almost everywhere, you see, yet not to Rome, for example. And had I been in Rome, I still might have missed the Pope. In short, I was overcome with an unquenchable thirst for something new, for a change of place, for overall, synthesized, panoramic impressions from a broad perspective. So what do you expect of me after such confessions? What shall I tell you? What shall I depict? A panorama, a vista? Something from a bird's-eye view? But the first thing you will say to me is that I have flown too high. Besides, I consider myself a conscientious man, and I would not lie by any means, not even as a traveler. Yet if I begin to depict and describe even a single panorama, then I am bound to lie, not because I am a traveler but simply because in my circumstances it is impossible not to lie. Judge for yourselves: Berlin, for instance, produced in me the most bitter impression, and I spent all of one day there. I know now that I am guilty before Berlin and that I would not dare to positively assert that it produces a bitter impression. Well, maybe bittersweet at any rate, but not just bitter. And what did my pernicious error result from? Surely from the fact that I, a sick man suffering from a liver ailment,[3] bounced along the railway for two days through rain and fog to Berlin; once arriving there, having gone without sleep, wan, tired, and worn out, I suddenly noticed at a glance that Berlin resembled Petersburg to an incredible degree. The same cordonlike streets, the same odors, the same . . . (but all the similarities cannot be counted!). "Oh, my God," I thought to myself. "Was it worth wearing myself out for two days in a train car just to see the same thing I left behind?" I did not even like the linden trees, but the Berliner would sacrifice all he holds dear for their preservation, perhaps even his constitution; and what is more dear to a Berliner than his constitution? On top of that, the Berliners themselves, to a man, looked so German that, without having even attempted to see the frescoes of Kaulbach (oh horror!), I quickly slipped away to Dresden, harboring in my soul a most profound conviction that getting used to Germans required a special effort and that if one is not used to them, they are extremely difficult to bear in large masses. In Dresden my offensiveness extended even to German women: as soon as I had gone out onto the street, I imagined that there was nothing more repulsive than the Dresden type of women and that even the singer of love himself, Vsevolod Krestovsky,[4] the most assured and cheerful of the Russian poets, would be completely at a loss here and would perhaps even doubt his calling. At that very minute, of course, I felt that I was talking nonsense and that under no circumstances could he ever doubt his calling. Within two hours everything became clear to me: having returned to my hotel room and stuck out my tongue before the mirror, I was convinced that my judgment on the ladies of Dresden was the blackest calumny. My tongue was yellow and malignant. . . . "Can it be, can it really be that man, this czar of nature, is dependent to such a degree on his very own liver?" I thought. "How base!" With these comforting thoughts I set out for Cologne. I admit that I was expecting a great deal from the Cathedral; I used to sketch it with reverence in my youth, when I was studying architecture. A month later, when I was passing through Cologne on my return trip from Paris and saw the Cathedral for the second time, I felt like "begging its forgiveness on my knees" for not perceiving its beauty the first time, for exactly the same reason Karamzin had fallen to his knees before the Rhine waterfall.[5] But, nonetheless, I did not like the Cathedral at all the first time: it seemed to me like lace, lace, nothing but lace, a haberdasher's knickknack resembling a paperweight for a writing desk about seventy sagenes high.* "Not very majestic," I decided, just as in the old days when our grandfathers decided in regard to Pushkin, "Writing comes too easily for him, nothing very lofty there." I suspect that two circumstances had an influence on this first decision of mine, the first being *eau de cologne*. Jean-Maria Farina[6] is located next to the Cathedral, and no matter what hotel you are staying in or what your mood might be, no matter how much you hide from your enemies and from Jean-Maria

---

*A sagene is equal to 2.134 meters or about seven feet.

Farina in particular, his patrons are sure to find you and shout, "*Eau de Cologne ou la vie,*" one or the other; there is no way out. I cannot state with too much certainty that they cry out precisely the words "*Eau de Cologne ou la vie,*" but who knows? Perhaps they do. I remember at the time I was constantly imagining and hearing things. The second circumstance which infuriated me and made me unfair was the new Cologne bridge. The bridge, of course, is magnificent, and the city has a right to be proud of it, but I felt that it was too proud. Needless to say, I immediately became angry about this. Besides, the penny collector at the entrance to the wondrous bridge had absolutely no right to take from me that reasonable toll, looking at me as if he were collecting a fine for some unknown offense I had committed. I do not know, but it seemed to me that this German was throwing his weight around. "He probably guessed that I am a foreigner and a Russian at that," I thought. His eyes, at least, were all but declaring, "You see our bridge, miserable Russian; well, you are a worm before our bridge and before every German because you do not have such a bridge." You will agree that this is offensive. The German, of course, never said any such thing, and perhaps it never entered his mind, but that does not matter: at the time I was so certain that this was precisely what he meant to say that I finally flew into a rage. "The devil take you," I thought. "We invented the samovar too . . . we have journals . . . we do things officers do . . . we have . . ." In a word, I was infuriated, and, after buying a bottle of *eau de cologne* (which I could not avoid), I immediately skipped off to Paris, hoping that the French would be much nicer and more entertaining. Now judge for yourselves: if I had controlled myself, if I had stayed in Berlin not a day but a week and the same in Dresden, let's say three days in Cologne or even just two, I probably would have taken a second or third look at the objects through different eyes and would have had a more proper notion of them. Even a sunbeam, a simple sunbeam, would have meant a great deal here: had a sunbeam shone on the Cathedral as one did on my second arrival in Cologne, the edifice would surely have appeared to me in its true light, and not as it did on that cloudy and even somewhat rainy morning, which was capable of arousing in me only an outburst of wounded patriotism. In no way, however, does it follow from this that patriotism rises up only in bad weather. And so you see, my friends, two and a half months are not enough to truly examine everything, and I am unable to provide you with the most accurate information. At times I must unwillingly tell a falsehood, and that is why. . . .

But here you stop me. You say that in this instance you do not need accurate information, that if needed you will find it in the *Reichard Guide,* and that, on the contrary, it would not be bad at all if every traveler sought not so much absolute accuracy (which is almost always beyond his powers to obtain) as absolute sincerity; he would not be afraid to sometimes reveal some personal impression or adventure of his, even though it might not bring him a great reputation, and he would not consult the renowned authorities to check out his conclusions. In a word, you require only my personal but sincere observations.

"Ah!" I exclaim. "So you require mere chatter, light sketches, personal impressions snatched on the run." I agree to this and shall consult the notes in my notebook right away. And I shall try to be as straightforward as I can. I ask you only to remember that there may be many mistakes in what I am now about to write for you. Of course, not all of it will be mistaken. It is impossible to be mistaken, for example, about the facts that Notre Dame and Bal Mabille are in Paris. The latter fact in particular has been so well certified by all the Russians who have written about Paris that it is now almost impossible to doubt it. In this, perhaps even I shall not be mistaken, but I offer no strict guaranty. After all, it is said that to be in Rome and not to see St. Peter's Cathedral is impossible. Well, judge for yourselves: I was in London and yet did not see St. Paul's. It's true, I didn't. I did not see St. Paul's Cathedral. There is a difference, of course, between Peter and Paul, but, all the same, it was rather improper for a traveler. There you have the first of my adventures which do not bring me a great reputation. (Well, I might have seen it from a distance of about two hundred sagenes, but I was in a hurry to get to Pentonville; I shrugged it off with a wave of my hand and rode on by.) But to the task, to the task! You know, don't you, that I did not spend the whole time just traveling around and taking a bird's-eye view. ("A bird's-eye view" does not mean "looking down on something." It is an architectural term, you know.) With the exception of eight days spent in London, I stayed in Paris for a whole month. So I shall write something for you in regard to Paris, because after all I did examine it more closely than I did St. Paul's Cathedral or the ladies of Dresden. Well, I begin.

2

In the Train Car

"The Frenchman has no common sense and would indeed consider it the greatest misfortune to have it." Fonvizin[1] wrote this sentence in the last century, and, my God, what pleasure he must have taken in writing it! I bet his heart was tickled with delight when he composed it. And, who knows, perhaps all of us since Fonvizin, for three or four generations on end, have read it not without a certain relish. Even now wherever they are encountered, all sentences like this, cutting foreigners down to size, contain something irresistibly pleasant for us Russians. Only on a profoundly secret level, of course, sometimes secret even from ourselves. Here echoes a certain vengeance for some wrong in the past. Perhaps this feeling is itself wrong, but I am somehow convinced that it exists in almost every one of us. We, of course, become abusive if suspected of this and become so without a trace of pretense; besides, I think Belinsky[2] himself was secretly a Slavophile in this sense. I remember that back then—fifteen years ago, when I knew Belinsky—I remember that the whole circle from that period bowed before the West, that is, mainly before France, with a reverence that approached oddity. France was in vogue then; this was in forty-six. It is not that they worshiped such names, for example, as George Sand, Proudhon, and others, or that they admired such figures as Louis Blanc, Ledru-Rollin, and so on.[3] No, they admired nothing but some pitiful excuses for

7

men, the most miserable names, who immediately prove to be scum when put to the test; these were the ones held in high esteem. And from them some great, imminent service to mankind was expected. A few of them were spoken of in that special whisper of reverence. . . . So what? I have never in my life met a man more passionately Russian than Belinsky, although, with the possible exception of Chaadaev,⁴ no one has been so boldly and at times so blindly indignant as he toward much of what is native to us; he apparently disdained everything Russian. I now think back and consider all this in the light of certain facts. So, who knows, perhaps at times Fonvizin's witticism did not seem very scandalous even to Belinsky. There are moments when even the finest, most legitimate tutelage is not particularly pleasing. Oh, for God's sake, do not suppose that to love one's native land means to abuse foreigners or that I think this. I do not think it at all and have no intention of thinking it, on the contrary, I even. . . . It is just a pity that I do not have time right now to explain more clearly.

By the way, aren't you thinking that instead of Paris I have started off with Russian literature? Am I writing a critical article? No, it is just that I have nothing else to do.

According to what is noted in my little book, I should now be sitting in a train car getting ready for tomorrow's arrival at Eydkuhnen, that is, for my first foreign impression, my heart pounding all the while. For this is where I shall finally see Europe, I who have been vainly dreaming of it for nearly forty years, I who, like Nekrasov's⁵ Belopyatkin, have

Longed to run off to Switzerland

since I was sixteen; but I did not run off, and now I am finally entering the "land of holy wonders," the land of my long yearnings and expectations, of my unyielding beliefs. "Lord, what kind of Russians are we?" flashed through my mind from time to time while I was on the train. "Are we in fact really Russians? Why does Europe create such a powerful, magical, alluring impression on us, no matter who we might be? That is, I am not speaking now of those Russians who have remained in Russia, those simple Russians whose name is fifty million, whom we hundred thousand to this day seriously regard as nobodies and whom our profound, satirical journals mock because they do not shave their beards. No, I am speaking now of our privileged upper class. You see, all, decidedly almost all, the development, science, art, civil consciousness, and humanity we have—all of it, all I say, comes from that land of holy wonders! You see, our whole life, from earliest childhood, has been geared to the European mentality. Is it possible that any of us could have prevailed against this influence, this appeal, this pressure? How is it that we have not been regenerated once and for all into Europeans? That we have not been so regenerated I think all will agree, some with joy, others, of course, with anger that we *have not grown up enough* for regeneration. But that is another matter. I am speaking only of the fact that we have not been regenerated even in the presence of such irresistible influences, and I cannot understand this fact. After all, our nursemaids and mamas have not protected us from this regeneration. It is truly both sad and laughable, you know, to think that had there been no Arina Rodionovna, Pushkin's nursemaid, then perhaps we would have had no Pushkin. This is nonsense, isn't it? Can it really be anything but nonsense? But what if, in fact, it is not nonsense? There are many Russian children now who are taken to France to be educated; what if another Pushkin were taken there and he had no Arina Rodionovna, not a word of Russian from the cradle? And there was no man as Russian as Pushkin! The son of a barin,* he saw into Pugechev[6] and penetrated the Pugachevian soul at a time when no one was penetrating anything. An aristocrat, he contained a Belkin[7] in his soul. Through his artistic power he renounced his environment and in Onegin pronounced a great judgment upon it from the viewpoint of the people's spirit. Indeed this was a prophet and a herald. Can it be that there is in fact some kind of chemical bond between the human spirit and its native soil, so that you cannot tear yourself away from it and, even if you do tear yourself away, you nonetheless return? After all, Slavophilism did not just drop down to us from the sky, and, although it later developed into a Moscow fancy, the basis for this fancy is broader than the Moscow formula and is perhaps rooted much deeper in some hearts than it seems at first glance. Indeed, perhaps even among the Muscovites it is rooted deeper than their formula. Oh, how difficult to express it clearly from the start even to oneself! Some vital, powerful thought is not made clear for three generations, so that its final form sometimes bears no resemblance to the original. . . ." And so in the train car on the way to Europe idle thoughts assailed me despite myself, partly,

---

*A member of the upper class in czarist Russia.

I admit, out of boredom and having nothing to do. One must be frank, you know! Up to now only those of us who have nothing to do have meditated on such subjects. Oh, how boring it is to sit idly on a train, just as it is boring for us in Russia to live without a pursuit of our own! Although they indulge you, take care of you, and sometimes pacify you until it seems you can stand it no longer, the anguish—yes, anguish—is still there precisely because you do nothing for yourself, because you are coddled too much; you just sit and wait until they get you to where you are going. Truly, if there were any more of it you would jump off the train and run alongside the locomotive on your own two legs. Even if the worst should happen, even if I should grow tired or get lost from want of activity, never mind! At least I move on my own two legs, at least I have found my own way and am doing it myself, at least if the cars collide and go flying into the air, I won't be locked in sitting idly and answering with my hide for someone else's mistake. . . .

God knows what comes into one's head in idleness!

Meanwhile night was coming on. They began lighting the lamps in the train cars. A husband and wife were situated opposite me, elderly people, landowners, and, it seemed, good people. They were hurrying off to an exhibition in London for just a few days and had left their family at home. To my right was a certain Russian who had spent ten years in London at the office of a commercial firm; he had just gone to Petersburg for two weeks on business and seemed to have completely lost all sense of longing for the homeland. To my left sat a pure, thoroughbred Englishman with a head of red hair parted in the English style and looking intensely serious. He did not utter even the slightest word to any of us in any language the entire way; during the day, without looking up, he read some sort of little book with that tiny English type which only Englishmen can tolerate and which they in fact praise for its convenience; and as soon as ten o'clock came in the evening, he immediately took off his boots and put on his slippers. Such was probably his routine his whole life, and he had no intention of changing his habits in the train car. Soon everyone dozed off; the whistle and the rattling of the train created an irresistible drowsiness. I sat thinking for a while and, I do not know why, the thought with which I began this chapter came to mind: "the Frenchman has no common sense." And do you know what? I feel an overwhelming urge to tell you, out of humanitarian feelings, about my meditations in the train car as we make our way to Paris: I was bored in the train car, you know, so now you will be bored. Other readers, however, ought to be spared, so I shall purposely insert all these meditations in a special chapter and call it *superfluous*. You, my friends, will labor over it, but others can discard it as superfluous. The reader must be addressed carefully and conscientiously, but with friends one may be direct. And so:

3

And a Completely
Superfluous One

By the way, these were not meditations but rather certain musings, random notions, even daydreams "about this and that but nothing in particular." First of all, I went back to the old days and especially contemplated the man who created the aphorism cited earlier about the Frenchman's common sense, and, for no special reason, I contemplated the aphorism itself. That man was a great liberal for his time. But, although throughout his life for some unknown reason he wore a French caftan, powder, and a little sword behind him to signify his knightly origin (which we have never had at all) and to defend his personal honor in Potemkin's[1] anteroom, he no sooner stuck his nose across the border than he began praying with all the biblical texts for deliverance from Paris and decided that "the Frenchman has no common sense," that he would even consider it the greatest misfortune. Incidentally, surely you do not think that I mentioned the little sword and the velvet caftan to reproach Fonvizin. Not a bit of it! Certainly it was not for him to wear a homespun coat, especially at a time when, as now, other gentlemen, in order to *be Russian* and blend with the people, did not wear homespun coats but contrived for themselves a ballet costume very much like the kind usually worn by the Uslads of Russian folk operas in love with their

Lyudmilas wearing kokoshniks.* Certainly not; at least the French caftan was at that time more understandable to the people: "A barin, you know, obviously does not look like a barin in a homespun coat." Not long ago I heard that a certain land-owner of our own day has also begun to wear the *Russian costume* in order to blend in with the people and to attend local meetings in it: as soon as they see him, they say to each other, "Who is that mummer hanging around here?" So you see, that landowner has not blended in with the people.

"No, as for me," another gentleman told me, "no, as for me, I shall not give an inch. I shall purposely shave my beard, and, if necessary, I shall go around in a dress coat. I shall attend to my affairs, but I shall show no sign that I want to fraternize. I shall be the master; I shall be stingy and prudent; I shall even be ruthless, an extortioner, if necessary. They will respect me more. After all, the main thing is to gain genuine respect from the start."

"Oh, go to the devil!" I thought. "It's as if he were plotting against some foreign enemy. Just like a war council."

"Yes," a third gentleman said to me, who, by the way, was most gracious. "I shall show up somewhere, and suddenly at one of their meetings they'll hand down a communal sentence for me to be flogged. What then?"

"And even if they did," I suddenly wanted to say, but I did not because I was afraid to. (What is this, why are we still afraid to express certain thoughts we have?) "Even if they did," I thought to myself, "even if they flogged you, so what? Among professors of aesthetics such turns of affairs are called the tragic elements in life and nothing more. Is that really reason enough to live isolated from everyone? No, if you're going to be with everyone, then be with them completely, and if you're going to be alone, then be completely alone. In other places people have suffered more than that, even weak women and children."

"For pity's sake, what do women and children have to do with it?" my adversary would have shouted at me. "The village would thrash me for no reason at all, over some cow that got into someone else's garden, and you take it to be a common concern."

"Well, yes, it's ridiculous, of course, the whole affair is such a ridiculous, sordid one that you don't want to soil your hands.

---

*A woman's headdress.

It's improper even to discuss it. Damn them all; let them all be whipped; after all, it's not me. For my part, I am ready to answer for the village's sentence no matter what: not a single birch rod would touch my sweet little squabbler, even if it were possible to dispose of him according to the village's sentence: 'Let's take money from him as punishment, brothers, because with him it's a question of nobility. He isn't used to it. As for us, we peasants have a backside made to be whipped,' the community would have decided in the words of the village elder in one of Shchedrin's[2] provincial sketches."

"Reactionary!" someone will shout upon reading this. "To stand up for the birch rod!" (I swear, someone will infer from this that I am standing up for the birch rod.)

"For goodness' sake, what are you talking about?" another will say. "You intended to talk about Paris, but you've gone over to birch rods. Where is Paris in all this?"

"Indeed, what is this?" a third will add. "You yourself write that you heard about all this not long ago, yet you did your traveling last summer. How could you have been thinking about all this at that time?"

"That really is a problem," I answer. "But allow me: after all, these are winter recollections of summer impressions. So the winter is mixed in with the summer. Not only that, I remember that as I was approaching Eydkuhnen, I was particularly pondering the thing in our fatherland which I was abandoning for Europe, and I remember that some of my reveries were in this spirit. I was specifically musing over the ways in which Europe has been reflected in us at various times and has imposed its civilization upon us, over the extent to which we have been civilized, and over exactly how many of us have been civilized so far. Now I myself see that all this is utterly superfluous. But I warned you that this whole chapter was superfluous. Incidentally, where was I? Ah, yes, the French caftan. That's what started it!"

Well, so one of these French caftans wrote *The Brigadier* then. *The Brigadier* was an astonishing thing for its day and produced an extraordinary effect. "Die, Denis, you will never write anything better," said Potemkin himself. Everyone began to stir as if waking from a sleep. "What? Can it be that even then," I continued my random musing, "people were already growing bored from having nothing to do, from walking around on someone else's leading strings?" I am not speaking only of the French suspenders of the day, and, by the way, I want to add that we are an extremely gullible nation and that it is all due to our good nature. We sit with nothing to do, for example, and all of a sudden we think someone has said something, done something, that we have caught the scent of our own spirit, that our calling has been found, and we all pounce on it, absolutely certain that now it begins. A fly goes by and we take it for an elephant. The inexperience of youth and with it a hunger of the spirit. This was beginning to happen just before *The Brigadier;* then, of course, it was only on a microscopic scale, but it continues unfailingly to this day: having found our calling, we squeal with delight. To squeal out and burst with delight is our first concern; then look, after a year or two we go our separate ways, heads hanging. Yet we do not grow tired, though we have begun a hundred times. As for others' suspenders, in Fonvizin's time almost no one, for the most part, doubted that these were the most sacred, the most European suspenders and the sweetest tutelage. To be sure, even now there are few who doubt. Our entire ultraprogressive party fervently stands up for foreign suspenders. But then, oh then, it was a time of such faith in all sorts of suspenders that it is amazing we did not move mountains, that our towering Alaunsky plateaus, the Pargolovo summits, and the Valdai peaks are still standing. It is true that a poet of that period mentioned a certain hero, saying that

He lies down on the mountains, the mountains crumble

and that

He throws towers over the clouds with his bare hands.[3]

But it seems that this was only a metaphor. Incidentally, gentlemen: I am now talking only about literature, specifically about belles lettres. Through it I would like to trace the gradual and beneficial influence of Europe on our fatherland. That is, it is impossible to imagine the kind of books that were published and read back then (up to and during the time of *The Brigadier*) without a certain joyful feeling of superiority on our part! Right now we have among us a particularly noteworthy writer, the charm of our age, one Koz'ma Prutkov.[4] His one shortcoming is an incomprehensible modesty: even now he still has not published his complete collected works. Well, a long time ago he once wrote in the miscellaneous column of the *Sovremenik* an item called "Notes from My Grandfather." Imagine what that plump, seventy-year-old grandfather of Catherine's day could have written at that time, having seen such sights, having been at court and at Ochakov,[5] and then returning to his estate to take up his memoirs. Now that must have really been interesting to write about! What that man had not seen! But, you know, everything he did consists merely of third-hand anecdotes like this one:

"*The Witty Reply of the Knight of Montbazon.* A young and extremely beautiful maiden once calmly asked the Knight of Montbazon in the presence of the King, 'My lord, which is attached to which, the dog to the tail or the tail to the dog?' And our Knight, being highly skilled in the art of clever rejoinder, replied without a hint of confusion but, on the contrary, in a steady voice, 'No one, Mademoiselle, is forbidden to take a dog by the tail or by the head.' This answer brought the King great satisfaction, and the Knight was not left without a reward."

You are thinking that this is a hoax, pure nonsense, that the world has never seen such a grandfather. But I swear to you that I myself personally read a little book from Catherine's time in my childhood, when I was ten years old, and in it I found the following anecdote. It attracted me so much that at the time I learned it by heart, and I have not forgotten it since:

"*The Witty Reply of the Knight of Rohan.* It is known that the Knight of Rohan had extremely bad breath. One day, while attending the levee of the Prince of Conde, the latter said to him, 'Move away, Knight of Rohan, for there is a foul smell coming from you.' To which the Knight immediately replied, 'It is not from me, all-merciful Prince, but from you, for you have just gotten out of bed.' "

That is, just imagine this landowner, an old warrior, perhaps with one arm missing, with an old wife, a hundred servants, and children like Mitrofan,[6] a man who goes to the bathhouse on Saturdays and steams himself into oblivion; and there he is, glasses on his nose, solemnly and with an air of importance spelling out such anecdotes, taking it all to be of the most genuine essence, almost as he regards his duties at work. And what a naive faith back then in the gravity and necessity of such news from Europe! "It is known," they say, "that the Knight of Rohan had extremely bad breath. . . ." Known to whom, why known, known to what bears in Tambov province? Who, indeed, even cares to know about it? But the grandfather is not concerned with such questions from free-thinkers. With the faith of a child he reasons that this "collection of witty words" is known to the court, and that is enough for him. Yes, indeed, at that time Europe came easily to us—in its physical form, needless to say. Morally, of course, there was no getting around the whip. We put on silk stockings and wigs, hung little swords on ourselves—and behold, we were Europeans. Not only was there nothing disturbing in all this, but it was even pleasant. But, in fact, everything remained as before: having set aside Rohan (about whom, incidentally, all that was known was that he had bad breath) and taken off our gloves, we dealt with our domestic servants, treated our families patriarchally, flogged the neighboring small landowner in the stables, and groveled in front of our superiors just as before. Even the peasant understood more about us: we despised him less, were less squeamish about his habits, knew more about him, were less foreign to him, less German. And if we put on airs in front of him, how could a barin not put on airs—that is a barin. And even if we flogged him to death, we were somehow nicer to the people than we are now because we were more a part of them. In a word, all these gentlemen were a simple, hardy people; they never made the slightest inquiries about anything; they took bribes, they flogged, they stole; they kowtowed with tender emotion and lived out their time richly and peacefully "in honest, childish depravity." I take it that these forefathers were not at all so naive, even with respect to the Rohans and Montbazons.

In fact, it could be that at times they were great rogues and had their own notions regarding all the European influences of the day coming from above. All this phantasmagoria, all the masquerading, all these French caftans, lace cuffs, wigs, little swords, all these plump, clumsy legs slipped into silk stockings, the soldier boys of the age with German wigs and boots—all of it, I think, was terrible knavery, the servile trickery of lackeys from below, such that even the people themselves sometimes noticed and understood it. Of course, it is possible to be a scrivener and a rogue and a brigadier and at the same time be most naively and touchingly certain that the Knight of Rohan was the "most sublime model of chivalry."[7] But, after, this did not prevent anything: the Gvozdilovs[8] nailed people to the wall as before; our Potemkin and everyone like him were ready to have our Rohans flogged in the stables; the Montbazons flayed the living and the dead; fists in lace cuffs and legs in silk stockings gave out slaps and kicks; and marquises loi-

tered around the courts
>Courageously sacrificing their necks.[9]

In a word, everything ordered and made to order from Europe at that time fit in very comfortably with us, beginning with Petersburg—the most fantastic city with the most fantastic history of all the cities on the face of the earth.

Well, things are not the same now, and Petersburg has had its effect. Now we have grown up and are fully European. Now even Gvozdilov himself maintains his skill when it comes to nailing someone to the wall, observes propriety, becomes a French bourgeois, and after a little while he will begin defending with the Scriptures the necesssity of buying and selling Negroes, as in the Southern states of North America. Such defenses using the Scriptures, moreover, are very much crossing over from the American states to Europe now. "So I'll go there and see it with my own eyes," I thought. You will never learn from books what you can see with your own eyes. And, incidentally, regarding Gvozdilov: why did Fonvizin give one of his most remarkable sentences in his *Brigadier* not to Sof'ya, the comedy's representative of noble and humane European development, but to the fool of a brigadier's wife, whom he fashioned not just as a simple fool but as a reactionary fool, so that everything she says is such utter nonsense and stupidity, it is as though it were not she but someone hidden behind her who speaks? Yet when it was necessary to speak the truth, the brigadier's wife nevertheless spoke of it, and not Sof'ya. After all, he made her not only an utter fool but even a bad woman; still, it is as if he feared and even considered it artistically impossible to have such a sentence leap out of the mouth of the well-bred, highly cultivated Sof'ya, as if he considered it more natural for a common, stupid female to utter it. Here is the scene, and it is worth recalling. It is extremely interesting precisely because it was written without any purpose or hidden meaning, naively and perhaps even accidentally. The brigadier's wife says to Sof'ya:

> In our regiment we had a captain of the first company by the name of Gvozdilov; his wife was such a pretty young thing. Well, it happened he would get mad about something, the more when he was drunk; then, as you believe in God, my dear, he nailed her to the wall, beat her, he did, till near nothing but her soul remained, and for no good reason. It was none of our business, but it was enough to make you cry just looking at her.

SOF'YA: Please, Madame, cease speaking of what is revolting to humanity.

BRIGADIER'S WIFE: You see, deary, you don't even want to *hear* about it; what must it have been for the captain's wife to *suffer* it?

Thus the well-bred Sof'ya with her highly cultivated sensitivity faded before a common woman. This is an amazing repartee (spoken in reproof) on the part of Fonvizin, and he wrote nothing more pointed, more humane, and . . . more accidental. And how many such highly cultivated progressives do we still have among our foremost figures who are extremely satisfied with their high cultivation and ask for nothing more? But the most striking thing of all is that Gvozdilov still nails his wife to the wall, and almost more comfortably than before. It's the truth. They say that it used to be done more from the heart and soul! The one I love, they say, is the one I'll beat. They say wives even worried when they weren't beaten: if he doesn't beat me, it means he doesn't love me. But all this is primitive, elemental, ancestral. Now this too has undergone development. Now Gvozdilov nails people to the wall almost on principle, and that is because he is still a fool, that is, a man of a time gone by who does not know the new system. With the new system one may do an even better job of taking command without the law of the fist. I expatiate on Gvozdilov now because to this day the most profound and most humane sentences are written about him. So much is written that even the public has grown sick of it. In spite of all the articles, our Gvozdilov is so alive that he is practically immortal. Yes, sir, he is alive and well, satiated and drunk. Now he is missing an arm and a leg and, like Captain Kopeikin,[10] "he has in a sense shed his blood." For a long time his wife has not been the "pretty, pretty young woman" she once was. She has aged, her face sunken and pale, furrowed with wrinkles and suffering. But when her husband and captain lay sick without an arm, she did not leave his bedside and spent sleepless nights over him, comforting him and weeping hot tears over him, calling him her sweet one, her brave fellow, her bright falcon, singing honors to his bold soldier's spirit. On the one hand, I know this is exasperating, I know! I know! But on the other hand: long live the Russian woman, for there is nothing better in our Russian world than her boundless, forgiving love. After all, isn't it true? All the more so now because when he is sober

Gvozdilov sometimes does not beat his wife, that is, not so often; he observes propriety and even says a tender word to her now and then. You see, he has begun to feel in his old age that he cannot manage without her; he is calculating, a bourgeois, and when he beats her now it is only in his drunkenness, according to his old habit, and then when he is in great sorrow. Well, this is progress, if you wish, and in it there is some consolation. And we are very fond of consolation. . . .

Yes, sir, now we have been completely consoled; we have consoled ourselves. So what if not everything around us now is still not very beautiful; we ourselves are so wonderful, so civilized, so European that even the people are ready to vomit from looking at us. The people now regard us as complete foreigners; they do not understand a single word, a single book, a single thought of ours—but, as you wish, that is progress. We now despise our people and native origins so deeply that we treat them with a new, unprecedented disgust such as did not even exist in the days of our Montbazons and Rohans; but, as you wish, that is progress. How self-assured we are, on the other hand, in our mission to civilize, how haughtily we solve problems, and what problems they are! There is no native soil, no people; nationality is merely a system of taxation; the soul is a *tabula rasa*, a piece of wax from which the real man can be immediately molded, the general, universal man, the homunculus—you need only apply the fruits of European civilization and read two or three books. And how serene, how majestically serene we are, since we doubt nothing and have solved and signed everything. With what serene self-satisfaction we have lashed out at Turgenev, for example, for daring not to be serene with us or satisfied with our majestic personalities, for refusing to accept them as his own ideal, for seeking something better than we. Better than we, for heaven's sake! What under the sun could be more beautiful and more flawless than we? Well, he caught it for Bazarov,[11] that sad, troubled Bazarov (the sign of a great heart), in spite of all his nihilism. We even lashed out at him for Kukshina,[12] for that progressive louse whom Turgenev combed out of Russian reality to show us, and we even added that he was going against the emancipation of women. And all this is progress, as you wish! Now standing over the people with a corporal's self-assuredness, like sergeant majors of civilization, we are a sight to behold: hands at our sides, eyes ablaze, looking like fops—we look like we are ready to spit: "What do you have to teach us, hoarse peasant, when all nationality, all national character, is reactionary

in essence, a means of distributing taxes and nothing more!"
Let us not give way to prejudices, for goodness' sake. Oh, my
God, by the way, now. . . . Gentlemen, let us suppose for a moment that I have already completed my journey and have returned to Russia. Allow me to relate an anecdote. One day this
autumn I picked up one of the most progressive newspapers.
I take a look: news from Moscow. Headline: "Remnants of Barbarism Remain" (or something of the sort, only very strongly
worded. It is a pity I do not have the newspaper in front of
me.) The story relates that a cab was seen one morning this
autumn in Moscow; in the cab sat a drunken matchmaker
dressed in ribbons and singing a song. The coachman was also
covered with bows, also drunk, also humming some tune! Even
the horse was in bows. Only I do not know whether or not it
was drunk too; probably drunk. In her hands the matchmaker
paraded a small parcel which she had brought from some new-
lyweds who had apparently spent a happy night. The parcel,
of course, contained a certain undergarment which, among the
common people, is usually shown to the parents of the bride
the next day. Looking at the matchmaker, the people laughed:
a lighthearted item. Indignantly, boastfully, sneeringly the
newspaper reported this unheard-of barbarism, "which remains even now, despite all the advances of civilization!"
Gentlemen, I confess to you that I burst out terribly with
laughter. Oh, please, do not think that I am defending primitive cannibalism, delicate undergarments, coverings, and so on.
This is vile, this is unchaste, this is savage, this is Slavic, I
know, I agree, although it was all done without any evil intention; on the contrary, it was with the aim of celebrating the
bride, in the simplicity of the soul, out of ignorance of anything
better, higher, European. No, I was laughing at something else.
Namely: I suddenly recalled our barin's wives and fashionable
shops. Of course, now civilized ladies no longer send dainty
garments to their parents; but when, for example, it comes to
ordering a dress from a milliner, with what tact, with what
fine calculation and a knowledge of their business do they insert padding into certain places in their charming European
clothing! What is this padding for? Why, it goes without saying,
for elegance, for aesthetics, *pour paraître.** . . . Not only that:
their daughters—those innocent, seventeen-year-old creatures
scarcely out of boarding school—even they know all about pad-

---

* For looks.

ding: what the padding is for, just where and in what spots this padding must be used, and exactly what purpose it all serves. . . . "Well," I thought with a laugh, "these cares, these worries, these *conscious* worries about padded accessories—are they more pure, more moral, more chaste than the unhappy delicate undergarment taken to the parents in simplehearted confidence, in the confidence that this is precisely what is required, what is moral. . . .!"

Oh, good heavens, do not think, my friends, that I am suddenly setting out to argue that civilization is not progress, but, on the contrary, in recent times in Europe it has stood over all progress with the whip and with prison! Do not think that I am about to demonstrate that among us civilization and the laws of true, normal development are barbarically mixed, to demonstrate that civilization has long since been condemned in the West itself and that there only the property owner stands up for it in order to save himself some money (although everyone there is a property owner or wants to be a property owner). Do not think that I am about to demonstrate that the human soul is not a *tabula rasa,* not a piece of wax from which the universal man may be molded; that nature is needed first of all, then science, then an independent, native, unconstrained life and a faith in one's own national strength. Do not think that I shall say to you, as if I didn't know, that our progressives (although far from all of them) do not at all promote padding and indeed hold it up to shame, as they do dainty garments. No, I only want to say one thing now: there was a reason why the article maligned and damned dainty garments, why it did not simply say that this is barbarism; it was obviously exposing the barbarism of the common people, a national, elemental barbarism, in contrast to the European civilization of our higher, well-bred society. The article had a swaggering tone, as though it did not care to acknowledge that the accusers themselves are perhaps a thousand times more vile and worse, that we have merely exchanged one set of prejudices and abominations for other, still great prejudices and abominations. It seemed that the article did not care to notice these, our own prejudices and abominations. Why, oh why, stand over the people like such a fop, hands at our sides and ready to spit . . .! This faith in infallibility and in the right to make such accusations is ridiculous, ridiculous enough to make you laugh. This is either faith or swaggering over the people or, ultimately, unreasoning, servile worship of European forms of civilization; in that case it is even more ridiculous.

ALBRIGHT COLLEGE LIBRARY 218296

Anyway, such cases are found a thousand times every day. Forgive the anecdote.

However, I am committing a sin. I really am committing a sin! It is because I have jumped from the grandfathers to the grandsons too soon. There were, indeed, interim periods. Remember Chatsky.[13] He is no native, roguish grandfather, no self-satisfied descendent who stands like a fop and has resolved everything. Chatsky is an altogether special type of our Russian European, the kind, enthusiastic, suffering type who appeals to Russia and the native soil and who nevertheless leaves again for Europe whenever he must seek

a place of refuge for injured feelings. . . .

In a word, he is now a completely useless type but at one time he was terribly useful. He is a phrase monger, a talker, but he is a sincere phrase monger who conscientiously feels miserable about his uselessness. Now he has been reborn in the new generation, and we believe in the strength of youth; we believe that he will soon appear again, no longer in hysterics as at Famusov's ball but as a conqueror, proud, mighty, gentle, and loving. At that time, moreover, he will realize that there is no refuge for injured feelings in Europe but perhaps right under his nose, and he will discover what to do and will set out to do it. And do you know what? I am certain that there are now among us not only master sergeants of civilization and European petty tyrants; I am certain, I maintain, that the young man has already been born . . . but more about that later. I still want to say a couple of words about Chatsky. There is only one thing I do not understand; after all, Chatsky is a very intelligent man. How did this intelligent man fail to find an occupation for himself? In fact, they all failed to find an occupation for two or three generations on end. This is a fact, and I think there is no point in speaking contrary to a fact, but one may ask out of curiosity. Well, then, I do not understand how an intelligent man cannot find an occupation for himself, no matter what the times or circumstances may be. This, they say, is a moot point, but in the depths of my heart I cannot believe it. Intelligence is for the purpose of obtaining what you want. If you cannot go a verst,* then go a hundred paces; it is much better to get closer to your goal, if you are moving toward

---

* 3,500 feet.

a goal. And if you want to immediately reach your goal in a single step, that, in my opinion, is not intelligence. Indeed, this is called downright laziness. We do not like difficulties; we are not accustomed to taking a step at a time; we think it better to fly to our goal in a single step or to become a Regulus.[14] Well, that is certainly white-handed laziness. Chatsky, however, did very well when he then slipped off abroad again; had he lingered a while, he might have set off for the East instead of the West. We love the West, love it, and everyone goes there when worse comes to worst. Well, here I am on my way there. *"Mais moi, c'est autre chose."** I saw them all there, that is, very many of them; you couldn't even count them all, and every one of them, it seems, is seeking a refuge for injured feelings. At least they are seeking something. The generation of Chatskys of both sexes after Famusov's ball, when the ball was generally over, has propagated itself there like the sands of the sea, and not only the Chatskys: they have all left Moscow to go there. How many Repetilovs are there, how many Skalozubs who have been retired and sent to the waters for their worthlessness. Natal'ya Dmitrievna and her husband are indispensable members there. Even Countess Khlestova is brought there each year. All of these ladies and gentlemen have even grown sick of Moscow. Molchalin is the only exception: he made other arrangements and stayed home; he alone stayed home. He has devoted himself to his fatherland, so to speak, to his native land. . . . Now you cannot lay a hand on him; now he will not even allow Famusov into his anteroom: "You see, we are neighbors in the country: in the city we don't even greet each other." He has found an occupation for himself in business affairs. He is in Petersburg and . . . and he has found success. "He knows Russia and Russia knows him." Yes, indeed, she knows him well and will not forget him for a long time. He does not even remain silent now; on the contrary, he is the only one who speaks. He knows best . . . but enough about him. I started to say of all of them that they seek a comforting refuge in Europe, and, it's true, I used to think they were better off there. Yet there is such sadness in their faces. . . . Poor people! And what wonted anxiety there is in them, what morbid, melancholy restlessness! They all go about with guidebooks and greedily throw themselves on every city to look at the curiosities, and, it's true, they do it as if it were an

---

*"But with me, it is a different manner."

obligation, as if they were performing a duty to the fatherland: they do not miss a single three-windowed palace if it is mentioned in the guidebook, not a single burgermeister's home, remarkably similar to the most ordinary Moscow or Petersburg home; they gape at a side of beef by Rubens and believe that it is the Three Graces because that is what the guidebook has ordered them to believe; they dash to the Sistine Madonna and stand before her in blank expectation: something will happen any second, someone will slip out from under the floor and dispel their meaningless melancholy and weariness. And they leave amazed that nothing happened. This is not the self-satisfied and completely mechanical curiosity of the English tourists who look more at their guidebooks than at the curiosities, expecting nothing new or amazing and verifying only whether the object is mentioned in the guidebook, how many feet high it is, and how many pounds it weighs. No, our curiosity is savage, nervous, ravenous, inwardly convinced beforehand that nothing will ever happen, until the first fly goes by, of course; once a fly has gone by, it means that something is about to begin again. . . .

I am speaking, you know, only of intelligent people now. There is no need to be concerned about the others: God always looks after them. Nor am I speaking of those who settle there once and for all, forget their language, and begin to listen to Catholic priests. Only this can be said about the whole bunch of us: we no sooner pass Eydkuhnen than we bear a striking resemblance to those unhappy little dogs who run about after having lost their master. You may well think that I am writing in mockery, accusing someone, that I am saying, "Look here, at the present time, when and so on, and you are abroad! The peasant problem rages, and you are abroad, and so on and so on!" Oh, nothing of the kind. Indeed, who am I to accuse? Accuse whom and for what? "We would be glad to do something, but there is nothing to do; and what there is, is done without us. The positions are filled, and no vacancies are anticipated. It's no good poking your nose in where it isn't wanted." Thus the excuse, and there is not much to it. We know the excuse by heart.

But what is this? Where have I wandered off to? Where could I have seen Russians abroad? After all, we are still coming to Eydkuhnen. . . . Or have we already passed it? Indeed, we have, and Berlin and Dresden and Cologne—we have passed them all. It is true, we are still in the train car, but before us is not Eydkuhnen; it is Erquelines, and we are entering France.

It is Paris, Paris, that's what I wanted to talk about after all, and I have actually forgotten! Instead, I have meditated at length on our Russian Europe; an excusable affair when you are yourself going to see European Europe. Besides, there is really no reason to beg your pardon. After all, my chapter is superfluous.

4

And Not Superfluous
for Travelers

A Final Resolution on Whether the
Frenchman Really "Has No Common Sense"

"But, no, really, why doesn't the Frenchman have any common sense?" I asked myself, examining four new passengers, Frenchmen, who had just entered our train car. These were the first Frenchmen I encountered on their native soil, not counting the customs inspectors at Erquelines, from which we had just set off. The customs inspectors were extremely polite; they did their work quickly, and I entered the train car very satisfied with my first step into France. Up to Erquelines, there were only two of us occupying our eight-seat compartment: myself and a Swiss, a simple and modest man, middle-aged, and a most pleasant conversationalist with whom I chatted continuously for two hours. Now, however, there were six of us, and, to my surprise, my Swiss friend suddenly became extremely reticent in the presence of our four new traveling companions. I turned to him to continue our previous conversation, but he seemed in a hurry to change the subject; he answered somewhat evasively, coldly, almost with anger, and turned toward the window to look at the scenery; a minute later he pulled out his German guidebook and was completely absorbed in it. I immediately gave up on him and silently studied our new traveling companions. They were rather strange people. They were traveling light and bore absolutely no resemblance to travelers. Not a bundle, not even a bit of clothing that in any way resembled a person on a trip. They were all in some sort of light frock coats, terribly shabby and threadbare, little better than those worn by our officers' orderlies or by the manor serfs in the country among our middle-class landowners. The linen on all of them was dirty, and their brightly colored ties were also dirty. Wrapped around one of them was the remnant of a silk kerchief of the type that is always worn and becomes saturated with a whole pound of grease after fifteen years of contact with the neck of the one wearing it. This same fellow, moreover, had some kind of cuff links with imitation diamonds the size of walnuts. Nevertheless, they all carried themselves with a certain style, even dashingly. All four appeared to be exactly the same age, thirty-five or so, and, though not exactly alike in the face, they were remarkably similar to one another. Their faces were wrinkled, with the insipid little French beards, also very similar to each other. It was obvious that, having been through various tribulations and forever mastering themselves, these people had acquired a sour but extremely businesslike facial expression. It also seemed to me that they were acquainted with one another, but I do not remember even a single word said among them. It was apparent that for some reason they did not want to look at us, that is, at the Swiss and me; casually whistling, casually sprawling on their seats, they indifferently but persistently looked out the windows of the coach. I lit a cigarette and, having nothing else to do, looked them over. It is true, a question flashed through my mind: what sort of people are these really? Certainly not workers, certainly not bourgeois. Could they be retired military men, sort of *à la demi-solde** or something of the kind? Somehow, though, I was not very concerned about them. After ten minutes, just as we came to the next station, all four of them, one after the other, immediately got off the train; the door slammed, and we rolled on. On this line they do not wait long at the stations; two minutes, maybe three, and they pull out. The service is splendid, that is, extremely fast.

As soon as we were left alone, the Swiss instantly slammed shut his guidebook, put it aside, and looked at me contentedly, with the obvious desire to continue our conversation.

"Those gentlemen did not stay long," I began, looking at him curiously.

"Yes, well, they only got on to go one station."

"Do you know them?"

"Them . . .? But they are policemen, you know."

---

*On half-pay.

"What? What do you mean policemen?" I asked, astonished.

"Just that. . . . I noticed right away that you didn't realize."

"And . . . they are actually spies?" (I still refused to believe it.)

"Why, of course; they got on because of us."

"You know this for certain?"

"Oh, there's no doubt about it! I've been through here several times before. We were pointed out to them back in customs when our passports were being read; they were given our names and so on. So they got on to accompany us."

"Yes, but why should they accompany us if they have already seen us? After all, you say we were pointed out to them back at the last station."

"Well, yes, and they were told our names. But that isn't much. Now they have studied us in detail: the face, dress, bags, in a word, everything about the way we look. They took note of your cuff links. You took out your cigarette case, and they noticed your cigarette case, in short, every little detail and peculiarity, every possible peculiarity. You could lose yourself in Paris; you could change your name (that is, if you were a suspicious character). Well, all of those little details can be of help in tracking you down. It's all being telegraphed to Paris this very minute from that station. There it will be kept for any situation that might arise. Not only that, the hotel proprietors must report all the details about foreigners, also down to the slightest trifle."

"But why were there so many of them? After all, there were four of them," I continued to ask, still a little perplexed.

"Oh, there are a lot of them here. This time there were probably only a few foreigners; if there had been more, they would have spread out through the train car."

"Pardon me, but they didn't so much as look at us. They were looking out the windows."

"Oh, don't worry, they examined everything. . . . They got on just for us."

"Well, well," I thought, "so this is how 'the Frenchman has no common sense.' " And (I am ashamed to admit it) I squinted at the Swiss rather distrustfully. "Perhaps you too, brother, know nothing about this but are only pretending," flashed through my head, but only for an instant, I assure you. It was absurd, but what are you going to do? Thoughts come involuntarily. . . .

The Swiss did not deceive me. At the hotel where I was staying they immediately noted all of my most minute features and reported them to the proper authorities. Judging from the precision and detail with which they examine you and describe your features, you might conclude that your entire subsequent life in the hotel, so to speak, your every step would be scrupulously observed and counted. The first time in a hotel, however, they did not trouble me much personally and took my description on the sly, except, of course, for those questions that they ask you according to the book in which you write down information about yourself: who, how, from where, with what intentions, and so on. But at the second hotel I stayed in, having lost my place in the first, the Hôtel Coquillière, after my eight days in London, they treated me much more frankly. This second one, the Hôtel des Empereurs, generally looked a bit more patriarchal in every respect. The proprietor and his wife really were very good people, extremely tactful, already an elderly couple, who were unusually considerate of their guests. On the very evening of the day I arrived there, the proprietor's wife caught me in the passageway and invited me into the room where the office was. Her husband was there too, but his wife, evidently, was in charge of everything concerning the business.

"Excuse us," she began very politely. "We need a description of you."

"But I've already informed you. . . . You have my passport."

"Yes, but . . . *votre état?*"*

This "*votre état*" is an extremely confusing thing, and it has been unpleasant for me everywhere. Well, what to write here? Traveler? Too vague. *Homme de lettres?*† They would have no respect for that.

"The best thing for us to write is *propriétaire;*‡ what do you think?" the proprietor's wife asked me. "That would be best of all."

"Oh, yes, that would be best of all," the husband nodded.

"So we have written it. And now: the reason for your coming to Paris?"

"As a traveler, passing through."

"Hm, yes, *pour voir Paris.*§ Allow me, monsieur: your height?"

"What do you mean my height?"

"I mean, exactly how tall are you?"

---

* Your profession.
† Man of letters.
‡ Proprietor, here meaning "landed gentry" or "landowner."
§ To see Paris.

"Medium, as you see."

"That is so, monsieur. . . . But it would be preferable to know more precisely. . . . I think, I think . . .," she continued, somewhat embarrassed, her eyes seeking advice from her husband.

"I think, *just so much,*" the husband decided, looking at me and estimating my height in meters.

"But why do you need this?" I asked.

"Oh, it is *in-dis-pen-sable,*" the landlady answered, obligingly stretching out the word *indispensable* and noting my height in the book all the same. "Now, monsieur, your hair? Blond, hm . . . a rather light shade . . . straight . . ."

And she made a note of my hair.

"Allow me, monsieur," she went on, putting down the pen, getting up from the chair, and coming toward me with a most amiable look. "Take two steps this way, toward the window. We must have a look at the color of your eyes. Hm, light. . . ."

And once again she looked to her husband for advice. Apparently they loved each other very much.

"More a shade of gray," the husband noted with a businesslike, even an anxious look. "*Voilà,*" he winked at his wife, pointing at something over his brow, but I understood perfectly well what he was pointing at. I have a little scar on my forehead, and he wanted his wife to note this distinguishing feature.

"And now allow me to ask," I said to the landlady when the whole examination was over. "Do they really demand such reports of you?"

"Oh, monsieur, it is in-dis-pen-sable . . . !"

"Monsieur!" her husband nodded with a particularly impressive air.

"But they didn't question me at the Hôtel Coquillière."

"That cannot be," the landlady quickly replied. "They could have much to answer for over that. They probably looked you over silently, but they certainly, most certainly, looked you over. We are more simple and open with our guests; we live with them as if they were our own relatives. You will be content with us. You'll see. . . ."

"Oh, monsieur!" the husband solemnly confirmed, and a look of tender emotion even appeared on his face.

Indeed, they were a most honest, most amiable couple, at least to the extent that I came to know them. Yet the word *indispensable* was not at all pronounced in any apologetic or demeaning tone but precisely with a sense of utter necessity, almost in keeping with their own personal convictions.

And so I am in Paris. . . .

5

Baal

And so I am in Paris. . . . Do not think, however, that I am going to tell you much about the city of Paris itself. I think you have read so much about it in Russian already that you must finally be sick of it. Not only that, you have been there yourselves and have probably noted everything better than I. And when I was abroad I really could not bear to see the sights according to the guidebook, according to the traveler's orders and obligations, and so I looked over things in other places such as I am ashamed to say. So I will not say exactly what I looked over, but to make up for it I will say this: I have formed a definition of Paris, attached an epithet to it, and I stand by that epithet. Namely: this is the most moral and most virtuous city in the whole world. What order! What prudence, what well defined and solidly established relationships; how secure and sharply delineated everything is; how content everyone is; how they struggle to convince themselves that they are content and completely happy; and how, in the end, they have struggled to the point where they really have convinced themselves that they are content and completely happy, and . . . and . . . they have stopped at that. The road goes no further. You will not believe that they have stopped at that; you will cry out that I am exaggerating, that this is all bitter patriotic slander, that in fact all this could not come to a complete stop. But after all, my friends, I did warn you in the first chapter of these notes that I would perhaps lie terribly. Don't bother me, then. You probably also know that if I lie, I lie in the conviction that I am not lying. As I see it, this is more than sufficient. So allow me some freedom, will you? Yes, Paris is a remarkable city. What comfort, what conveniences of every kind for those who have a right to conveniences, and, again, what order, what a *calm of order,* so to speak. I keep coming back to the order. Truly, with a little more, Paris and its million and a half residents will turn into some kind of professorial German town fossilized in calm and order, the kind that Heidelberg is, for example. Somehow it is being drawn in that direction. And couldn't there be a Heidelberg of colossal dimensions? And what regimentation! Understand me: not so much external regimentation, which is unimportant (comparatively, of course), but a colossal internal, spiritual regimentation stemming from the soul. Somehow Paris is willingly growing narrow, diminishing with love, huddling with tender emotion. In this respect it is nothing like London, for example. I was in London all of eight days, and, outwardly at least, that vast scenery, those bright layouts, distinctive and unregulated by any one measure, have left their mark on my impressions. Everything is so huge and abrupt in its individuality. This individuality can even be deceptive. Every abruptness, every contradiction, gets along with its antithesis and stubbornly walks hand in hand with it; they contradict each other yet apparently in no way exclude each other. It seems that they all stubbornly stand up for themselves and live in their own way, yet they apparently do not bother each other. At the same time, there is a stubborn, blind, already inveterate struggle here, a struggle to the death between the general individualistic basis of the West and the necessity of somehow getting along with each other, of somehow putting together a community and settling into a single anthill;[1] it may turn into an anthill, but if only we settle into it without devouring each other, then we won't turn into cannibals! In this regard, on the other hand, the same thing may be noted as in Paris: the same desperate struggle to maintain the status quo out of despair, to tear from oneself all desires and hopes, to curse one's future, and to bow down to Baal.[2] But please do not be carried away by high-sounding language; all this is consciously noted only in the souls of advanced thinkers and unconsciously, instinctively, in the vital functions of all the masses. But the bourgeois, in Paris for example, is consciously almost quite content and is convinced that everything is as it should be, and he will even thrash you if you doubt that everything is as it should be; he will thrash you because he is still afraid of something, in spite of all his self-confidence. It is the same in London, but what vast, overwhelming scenes! Outwardly what a difference from Paris! A city bustling day and night, as immense as the sea; the screeching and howling of machines; the railroads built over the houses (and soon under the houses); that boldness of enterprise; that seeming disorder which in essence is bourgeois order in the highest degree; that polluted Thames; that air saturated with coal dust; those magnificent public gardens and parks; those dreadful sections of the city like Whitechapel with its half-naked, savage, and hungry population. A city with its millions and its worldwide trade, the Crystal Palace, the International Exposition. . . . Yes, the Exposition is striking. You feel a terrible force that has united all these people here, who come from all over the world, into a single herd; you become aware of a gigantic idea; you feel that here something has already been achieved, that here there is victory and triumph. You even begin to be afraid of something. No matter how independent you might be, for some reason you become terrified. "Hasn't the ideal in fact been achieved here?" you think. "Isn't this the ultimate, isn't it in fact the 'one fold'? Isn't it in fact necessary to accept this as the truth fulfilled and grow dumb once and for all?" It is all so solemn, triumphant, and proud that you begin to gasp for breath. You look at these hundreds of thousands, these millions of people humbly streaming here from all over the face of the earth— people who come with a single thought, peacefully, persistently, and silently crowding into this colossal palace—and you feel that here something final has been accomplished, accomplished and brought to an end. It is a kind of biblical scene, something about Babylon, a kind of prophecy from the Apocalypse fulfilled before your very eyes. You feel that it would require a great deal of eternal spiritual resistance and denial not to succumb, not to surrender to the impression, not to bow down to fact, and not to idolize Baal, that is, not to accept what is as your ideal. . . .

"Oh, this is nonsense," you will say, "morbid nonsense, nerves, exaggeration. No one would stop at this, and no one would take this to be his ideal. Besides, hunger and slavery are no one's friends, and, more than anything else, they will stir up negation and engender skepticism. But well-fed dilettantes out strolling for their own pleasure, of course, can create scenes from the Apocalypse and amuse their nerves, exaggerating and extorting from every phenomenon powerful sensations for their own excitement. . . ." Very well, I answer, let us suppose that I got carried away with embellishment, just so. But if you were to see how proud is that mighty spirit which created this colossal embellishment and how proudly convinced this spirit is of its victory and its triumph, then you would shudder at its pride, its persistence, and its blindness, shudder for those over whom this proud spirit hovers and rules. In the presence of such enormity, in the presence of such gigantic pride in the sovereign spirit, in the presence of the triumphant finality of that spirit's creations, even the hungry soul often comes to a standstill, grows humble, bows down, seeks salvation in gin and depravity, and begins to believe that everything is as it should be. Fact weighs heavy; the masses grow numb and wander about like zombies; or if skepticism arises, dismally and with a curse they seek salvation in something like Mormonism. And in London you can see the masses in such dimensions and under such conditions as you will see nowhere else in the world in all your waking hours. I have been told, for example, that on Saturday nights half a million workers, male and female, and their children flood the entire city like a sea, gathering mostly in certain quarters, and celebrate the Sabbath all night until five in the morning; that is, they stuff themselves and get drunk, like animals, to last the whole week. All this costs them their weekly savings, everything earned by heavy labor and malediction. In the butcher shops and food stores gas lights burn in thick clusters, brightly illuminating the streets. It is as if a ball were being given for those white Negroes. The people crowd the open taverns and streets. This is where they eat and drink. The drinking establishments are decorated like palaces. Everyone is drunk, not with cheer but dismally, miserably, and, in a rather strange way, silently. Only now and then do swearing and bloody brawls disturb this suspicious silence that arouses sorrow in you. Everyone rushes as fast as he can to drink until he loses consciousness. . . . The wives do not fall behind their husbands but get drunk with them; the children run and crawl among them. On such a night at two o'clock I once got lost and for a long time roamed the streets in the midst of the numberless crowd of dismal people, inquiring about the way by making signs, for I do not know a word of English. I found my way, but the impression of what I saw tormented me for three days afterward. People are people everywhere, but here everything was so colossal, so bright that it is as if you were feeling what until now you had only imagined. Indeed, here you do not even see the people but a loss of consciousness, systematic, submissive, encouraged. And, looking upon all these pariahs of society, you feel that for a long time yet the prophecy will not come true for them, that for a long time yet they will not be given palm leaves and white garments, and that for a long time to come they will appeal to the throne of the Most High, "How long, oh Lord?" And they themselves know this and meanwhile avenge themselves against society as some kind of underground Mormons, Shakers, wanderers. . . . We are surprised at the stupidity of going over to the Shakers and becoming wanderers; we do not even suspect that here is a secession from our social formulas; a stubborn, unconscious secession; an instinctive secession, no matter what the cost, for the sake of salvation; a secession from us made with disgust and horror. These millions of people, abandoned and driven away from the human feast, shoving and crushing each other in the underground darkness into which they have been thrown by their older brothers, gropingly knock at any gate whatsoever and seek entrance so they won't suffocate in the dark cellar. It is a final, desperate attempt to form their own group, their own crowd, and to separate themselves from everything, even from the human image, if only to be something of their own, if only to avoid being with us. . . .

In London I saw another mass of people, the dimensions of which you will see nowhere except in London. The embellishments were there too, after their own fashion. Whoever has been in London has surely at least once gone to Haymarket at night. At night prostitutes crowd several streets in this quarter by the thousands. The streets are illuminated by clusters of gas lights, the like of which we cannot comprehend. At every step there are magnificent coffee houses ornamented with mirrors and gold. Here are the meeting places, here the refuges. It is even terrifying to enter this crowd. And how strange is its composition. There are old women and beautiful women, before whom you would stop in awe. In all the world there are no women more beautiful than English women. They pack the dense, cramped streets with difficulty. The crowd does not keep to the sidewalks but flows over the entire street. It thirsts for its prey and throws itself with shameless cynicism on the first person it meets. Here are sparkling, expensive clothes and near rags and extreme differences in age gathered all together. The drunken tramp elbows his way through this terrible crowd, and the titled wealthy man comes by here too. Swearing, arguing, shouting, and the soft, whispering summons of a beautiful, still-timid woman are heard. And sometimes what beauty!

The faces are like those in keepsakes. I remember that I once dropped by a certain casino. The music was blaring, dancers were moving about, and a huge number of people was crowding the place. The decor was magnificent. But the Englishman's dismal character does not leave him even in the midst of gaiety: they dance seriously, even sadly, hardly going through the steps, as if it were an obligation. Above, in the gallery, I saw a girl and stopped in utter awe: I have never encountered anything like such an ideal of beauty. She was sitting behind a small table with a young man who seemed to be a wealthy gentleman and, by all indications, was not a regular patron of the casino. Perhaps he had been looking for her, and they finally met or agreed to meet here. He spoke with her little and somewhat abruptly, as if it were something they did not want to talk about. The conversation was frequently interrupted by long periods of silence. She too was very sad. Her facial features were soft and delicate; there was something secret and sad in her lovely and rather proud stare, something pensive and melancholy. I think she was consumptive. She was, she could not help but be, higher than this whole crowd of unhappy women in her breeding; what else does the human face mean? Nevertheless, she was drinking gin here, for which the young man had paid. He finally got up, squeezed her hand, and they parted. He left the casino, and, blushing, with deep patches on her pale cheeks aflame from the liquor, she went and lost herself in the crowd of women earning a living. In Haymarket I noticed mothers who were bringing their young daughters into the business. Little girls around twelve years of age take you by the hand and ask you to go with them. I remember in the crowd of people on the street I once saw a little girl not more than six years old, all in rags, filthy, barefooted, hollow-cheeked, and beaten: her body was covered with bruises that could be seen through her rags. She walked as though unconscious of herself, without hurrying, going nowhere, wandering, God knows why, in the crowd; perhaps she was hungry. No one paid any attention to her. But what struck me most of all was that she walked with a look of such sorrow, of such hopeless despair, on her face that to see this little creature, already crushed by such malediction and despair, was somehow unnatural and terribly painful. She continually rocked her dishevelled head from side to side as though pondering something; she drew her little arms apart, making gestures with them, and then brought them together and pressed them to her half-naked chest. I turned around and gave her a half-shilling. She took the silver coin and then wildly, with frightened astonishment, looked into my eyes and suddenly took to her heels as fast as her legs could go, as if afraid that I would take the money away from her. Generally playful subjects. . . .

And then one night in a crowd of those lost women and profligates, a woman who was hurriedly making her way through the crowd stopped me. She was dressed all in black, with a hat that almost covered her face; I practically had no time to examine it; I remember only her fixed gaze. She said something in broken French that I could not make out, slipped some little piece of paper into my hand, and quickly went on. By the light of a coffee house window I looked over the piece of paper: it was a small, square scrap; on one side were printed the words "*Crois-tu cela?*"* And on the other side, also in French: "I am the resurrection and the life . . ." and so on—a few well-known lines. You will agree that this too is rather original. It was later explained to me that this was Catholic propaganda poking its nose into everything, persistent and tireless. Sometimes they distribute these pieces on the street, sometimes booklets consisting of various passages from the Gospels and the Bible. They distribute them free of charge, forcing them on you, shoving them into your hands. There is a huge number of these propagandists, men and women. This propaganda is subtle and calculating. The Catholic priest himself will track down and force his way into the poor family of some worker. He will find, for example, a sick man lying in a pile of straw on a damp floor, surrounded by children crazed with hunger and cold and by a hungry and often drunk wife. He will feed and clothe all of them, bring them heat, set about treating the sick man, purchase medicine, become a friend to the household, and end up by converting them all to Catholicism. Sometimes, however, after a recovery, they drive him away with curses and blows. He does not give up and goes on to someone else. They too throw him out; he will endure everything and will ultimately catch someone. The Anglican priest, on the other hand, will not go to the poor. The poor are not even allowed in the church because they have nothing with which to pay for a place on the bench. Marriages among the workers and the poor in general are very often illegal because church weddings are expensive. Many of these husbands, incidentally, horribly beat their wives, mutilate them to the point of death, mostly with pokers made for stirring coals. For them, this is some sort of instrument designed for beating. At least in the papers

---

*Do you believe in this?

describing family quarrels, maimings, and murders, a poker is always mentioned. Their children, when hardly adolescents, often go out into the street, mingle with the crowd, and in the end do not return to their parents. Anglican priests and bishops are proud and wealthy, live in rich parishes, and grow fat with their consciences completely at peace. They are great pedants, highly educated, and with an air of importance seriously believe in their stupid moral dignity, in their right to moralize calmly and with self-assurance, to grow fat and live for the wealthy. It is a religion of the rich and wears no mask. At least it is rational and free of deception. Convinced to the point of stupefaction, these professors of religion have their own form of amusement: missionary work. They go all over the earth, penetrate into the depths of Africa, to convert a single savage and forget about the millions of savages in London who have nothing to pay them. But the rich Englishmen and all the golden calves in general are extremely religious, dismally, morosely, and peculiarly so. Since the beginning of time English poets have loved to sing of the beauty of the provincial pastors' dwellings shaded by hundred-year-old oaks and elms, of their virtuous wives and the ideal beauty of their blond daughters with blue eyes.

But when the night passes and the day begins, the same proud and dismal spirit again regally hovers over the gigantic city. He is not troubled by what has been during the night; he is not troubled by what he sees around himself during the day. Baal reigns and does not even demand submission because he is sure of it. His faith in himself is limitless; he contemptuously and calmly gives out organized charity, just to get rid of it, and it is impossible to shake his self-confidence. Baal does not conceal from himself, as they do in Paris for example, the savage, suspicious, and disturbing phenomena of life. The poverty, suffering, grumbling, and torpor of the masses do not trouble him in the least. He contemptuously allows all these suspicious and ominous phenomena to live along with his own life, at his side, in the open. He does not make a cowardly attempt, as the Parisian does, to reassuringly convince himself, to hearten and tell himself, that everything is peaceful and prosperous. He does not hide away the poor somewhere, as in Paris, so they will not disturb or vainly frighten away his sleep. Like ostriches, the Parisians like to hide their heads in the sand, so as not to see the hungers. In Paris. . . . But there I go again! Once more, I am not in Paris. . . . When, Lord, will I accustom myself to order . . .?

6

An Essay Concerning
the Bourgeois

Why is he all huddled up here? Why does he want to turn himself into small change, to be shy, to shrivel up? "I'm not here, I'm not in the world at all; I've hidden myself, pass by, please, go by without noticing me, pretend you don't see me, pass on by, pass on by!"

"But whom are you talking about? Who is huddled up?"

"Why, the bourgeois."

"He's king, for goodness' sake, he's everything, *le tiers état c'est tout,*[1] and you claim he is huddled up!"

Indeed I do. Why did he hide behind the Emperor Napoleon? Why at the Chamber of Deputies did he forget the high style that he had loved so much before? Why does he not want to remember anything, and why does he throw up his hands when reminded of anything that was in the old days? Why is there suddenly alarm in his mind, in his eyes, and on his tongue when others dare to desire something in his presence? Why, when he desires something for himself in a moment of capricious foolishness, will he immediately flinch and begin to disavow it—"Lord, what am I doing!"—and for a long time afterward conscientiously attempt to expiate his behavior with diligence and obedience? Why does he look as though he is saying, "Here, I'll do a little business in my shop today, and, God willing, I'll do business again tomorrow and perhaps the day after tomorrow, by the grace of the Lord. . . . Well, and

43

then, then, if only I can quickly save up just a little bit, and—
après moi le déluge"? Why does he put all the poor away somewhere and make believe they do not exist at all? Why is he
satisfied with banal literature? Why does he terribly want to
convince himself that his journals are incorruptible? Why does
he agree to give so much money to spies? Why does he not dare
to utter a word about the Mexican expedition?[2] Why are husbands portrayed in the theatre as being so noble and rich, while
the lovers are all such ragamuffins, without position and pa-
tronage, some kind of shop clerks or artists, rotten to the utmost degree? Why does he fancy that all the wives, to a one,
are absolutely faithful, that the foyer is flourishing, that the
pot-au-feu is boiled on a most virtuous fire, and that her coiffure is in the best style one could possibly imagine? Regarding
the coiffure, the matter has been resolved, long settled, without
any discussion, has settled itself; and even though every minute cabs drive along the boulevards with their shades drawn,
even though everywhere there are hideaways for all the interesting needs, even though the wives' dresses are often much
more expensive than one would imagine they could be, judging
from what the husbands can afford, it has been resolved, signed,
and sealed, and what more could you want? And why has it
been resolved, signed, and sealed? Indeed, this is why: if it
were not so, then they might think that the ideal had not been
attained, that in Paris there is still no perfect earthly paradise,
that there might be something more to desire, that therefore
the bourgeois himself is not completely satisfied with the order
for which he stands and which he forces on everyone, that there
are rifts in society which must be mended. That is why the
bourgeois smears the little holes in his boots with ink lest, God
forbid, anyone notice them! And the wives eat candy and wear
gloves, so that the Russian ladies in distant Petersburg envy
them to the point of hysterics; they show their little feet as
they most gracefully raise their dresses on the boulevards.
What more is needed for complete happiness? Hence titles of
novels such as *The Wife, the Husband, and the Lover* are no
longer possible under these conditions, for there are no lovers,
nor can there be. And if there were as many of them in Paris
as there are grains of sand in the sea (and perhaps there are
even more), there still are none nor can there be, because
everything has been resolved, signed, and sealed, because
everything shines with virtue. It is necessary that everything
shine with virtue. Looking at the great courtyard of the Palais
Royal in the evening, up to eleven o'clock, one must certainly

shed a tear of tender emotion. Countless husbands stroll arm in arm with countless wives; their sweet and well-behaved little children frolic all around; a little fountain babbles, and the monotonous splashing of its stream reminds you of something peaceful, quiet, eternal, constant, Heidelbergian. And, to be sure, there is not just one little fountain in Paris that babbles so; there are many little fountains, and everywhere it is the same, so that the heart rejoices.

The demand for virtue in Paris is unquenchable. Today the Frenchman is serious, solid, and often his heart is even deeply moved, so that I do not understand why he is still in terrible dread of something, in dread despite all the *gloire militaire* which thrives in France and for which Jacques Bonhomme* has paid so dearly. The Parisian passionately loves to trade, but it seems that in trading and peeling you like a lime in his store, he does not peel you simply for profit, as he once did, but out of virtue, out of some sort of sacred duty. To amass a fortune and possess as many things as possible has become the primary code of morality, a catechism, of the Parisian. It was that way before, but now, now it has taken on a certain sacred aspect, so to speak. Formerly something besides money was acknowledged, so that a man without money but who had other qualities could count on at least some kind of respect; but now none at all. It is necessary to accumulate money and acquire as many things as possible, and only then can one count on any kind of respect. And not only the respect of others but even self-respect cannot be counted on in any other way. The Parisian does not think himself worth a penny if he feels that his pockets are empty, and he feels it consciously, conscientiously, and with great conviction. You are allowed amazing things, if only you have money. Poor Socrates is merely a stupid, harmful phrasemonger and is respected only on the stage, for the bourgeois still likes to respect virtue on the stage. A strange person, this bourgeois: he openly proclaims that money is the highest virtue and human obligation, but at the same time he passionately loves to playact, especially as one of the higher nobility. All Frenchmen have a remarkably noble look. The most vile Frenchman, who for a farthing would sell you his own father and without even being asked would add something else to the bargain, has at the same time, even at the very moment he is selling you his father, such an imposing bearing that you are overcome with bewilderment. Enter a store to buy some-

---

*The French "John Doe."

thing, and the lowest salesclerk will crush you, simply crush you with his ineffable nobility. These are the very salesclerks who serve as models of the most sublime chivalry for our Mikhailovsky Theatre. You are overwhelmed; you simply feel guilty before these salesclerks. You come to spend, say, ten francs, yet you are greeted like Lord Devonshire. For some reason you become terribly ashamed; you want to quickly assure him that you are not Lord Devonshire at all but just who you are, a modest tourist who came in to buy something for only ten francs. But the young man with a most happy appearance and ineffable nobility of soul, at the sight of whom you are ready to confess yourself a scoundrel (because he is at such a level of nobility!), begins to show you merchandise worth tens of thousands of francs. In a single minute he has covered the whole counter for you, and it occurs to you that he, the poor fellow, will have to put it back again on your account, he, Grandison, Alcibiades, Montmorency; and on whose account? On your account; you, who with your unenviable appearance, your vices and deficiencies, and your disgusting ten francs have the impudence to disturb such a marquis—as soon as you realize all that, willy-nilly, in an instant, standing right there at the counter, you begin to despise yourself to the utmost. You are filled with remorse and curse fate because right now you have only a hundred francs in your pocket; you toss them out, your eyes asking for forgiveness. But he magnanimously wraps up for you the item purchased with your miserable hundred francs, forgives you for all the trouble and disturbance you have caused in the store, and you beat your retreat as quickly as possible. Arriving home, you are terribly surprised to find that you had intended to spend only ten francs but had spent a hundred. How many times, walking along the boulevard or the Rue Vivienne where there are so many huge haberdasheries, have I mused to myself, "If ever the Russian ladies were to come here. . . ." But the salesmen and elders in the Orel, Tambov, and various other provinces know what would follow better than anyone. When in stores, Russians generally have a burning desire to show that they have immense sums of money. On the other hand, there is such shamelessness in the world, as among Englishwomen for example, who not only are not embarrassed that some Adonis or William Tell has covered a whole counter with merchandise for them but who even begin—oh, horror!—to haggle over ten francs. But William Tell does not miss his mark: he will avenge himself, and for a shawl worth fifteen hundred francs he will milk twelve thousand from milady, and in such a way that she will remain completely satisfied. But in spite of this, the bourgeois has a passionate love for ineffable nobility. At the theatre, be sure you show him characters uninterested in money. Gustave must shine with nobility alone, and the bourgeois will weep with tender emotion. Without ineffable nobility he cannot even sleep peacefully. But taking twelve thousand instead of fifteen hundred francs was a duty: he took it for the sake of virtue. Stealing is vile, base—for this it's the galleys; the bourgeois is prepared to forgive a great deal, but he will not forgive stealing, even if you or your children are dying of hunger. But if you steal for the sake of virtue, oh, then everything is completely forgiven. For you simply want to *faire fortune* and accumulate many things, that is, fulfill the duty of nature and humanity. That is why the points on stealing for a base purpose, that is, for a crust of bread, and on stealing for a lofty virtue are clearly defined in the code. The latter is protected to the utmost, encouraged, and unusually solidly organized.

Why then—once again I am back where I started—why then is the bourgeois still somehow afraid of something, as if he were upset about something? What worries him? Braggarts, phrasemongers? But, after all, he now sends them to the devil with one swift kick of his leg. The arguments of pure reason? But, after all, reason has proven untenable in the face of reality; indeed, the very wisest, most learned of men are now beginning to teach that there are no arguments of pure reason, that nowhere in the world does pure reason exist, that abstract logic is not applicable to mankind, that there is the reason of the Johns, the Peters, the Gustaves, but there has never been any pure reason; it is merely an unfounded invention of the eighteenth century. Whom then do they fear? The workers? But, after all, the workers are also proprietors at heart: their whole ideal lies in being proprietors and acquiring as many things as possible; such is their nature. A nature does not appear from nowhere. All this is cultivated over the centuries and developed over the centuries. A nationality is not easily altered; it is not easy to abandon the habits of centuries, ingrained in the flesh and blood. The farmers? But, after all, the French farmers are arch-proprietors, the most narrow-minded proprietors, that is, the best and most complete ideal of the proprietor that can be imagined. The communists? The socialists, finally? But these people have squandered away most of their time, and in his soul the bourgeois deeply despises them; he despises them, yet he nevertheless fears them. Yes, even now he fears these people. But why, really, is he afraid? After all, Abbot Sieyès[3] predicted in his famous pamphlet that the

bourgeois would be *everything:* *"What is the tiers état? Nothing.
What should it be? Everything."* Well, what he said has come
to pass. Of all the words spoken at that time, these words alone
have come true; they alone have remained true. But for some
reason the bourgeois still does not believe, in spite of the fact
that everything said after Sieyès's words has faded and burst
like a soap bubble. Indeed, it was shortly after his *liberté, égalité, fraternité* was proclaimed. Liberty. What liberty? Equal liberty for everyone to do anything he wants to within the limits
of the law. When may you do anything you want to? When you
have millions. Does liberty give each person a million? No.
What is the person without a million? The person without a
million is not the one who does anything he wants to but the
one with whom they do anything they want. And what follows
from this? It follows that besides liberty there is still equality,
namely equality before the law. Regarding this equality before
the law, it may only be said that, in the manner in which it is
now applied, every Frenchman can and must take it as a personal insult. What remains of the formula? Brotherhood. Well,
this is a very curious point, and it must be admitted that it
continues to form the chief stumbling block for the West. Western man speaks of brotherhood as the great motivating force
of mankind and does not realize that nowhere is brotherhood
achieved if it does not exist in reality. What is to be done?
Brotherhood must be created no matter what. But it turns out
that brotherhood cannot be created because it creates itself, is
given and found in nature. But in the French nature—to be
sure, in the Western nature in general—it has not shown up;
what has shown up is a principle of individuality, a principle
of isolation, of urgent self-preservation, self-interest, and self-
determination for one's own *I,* a principle of the opposition of
this *I* to all of nature and all other people as a separate and
autonomous entity completely equivalent and of equal value
to everything that exists outside itself. Well, brotherhood could
not come from such a self-conception. Why? Because in brotherhood, in true brotherhood, it is not the separate personality,
not the *I,* that must plead for the right to its own equality and
equal value with *everyone else,* but rather this *everyone else*
must *on its own* come to the one demanding his right to individuality, to this separate *I,* and on its own, without his asking,
must recognize his equality and equal value to itself, that is,
to everyone else in the world. This very rebellious and demanding individual, moreover, must above all sacrifice all of
his *I,* his entire self, to society, and not only without demanding

his rights but, on the contrary, giving them up to society unconditionally. But the Western personality is not used to such a turn of affairs: it demands with the use of force, demands its rights; it wants *to be separate*—and so brotherhood does not come. Of course, it may be regenerated. But it takes thousands of years to accomplish this regeneration, for such ideas must first enter into the flesh and blood in order to become a reality. What, you will say to me, must one be void of personality in order to be happy? On the contrary, on the contrary, I say; not only is the absence of personality not necessary but one must precisely become a personality on a much higher level than that which is now defined in the West. Understand me: voluntary, completely conscious self-sacrifice imposed by no one, sacrifice of the self for the sake of all, is, in my opinion, a sign of the very highest development of the personality, of the very height of its power, the highest form of self-mastery, the greatest freedom of one's own will. To voluntarily lay down one's life for the sake of all, to go to the cross or to the stake for the sake of all, can be done only in the light of the strongest development of the personality. A strongly developed personality, fully convinced of its right to be a personality, no longer having any fear for itself, cannot do otherwise because of its personality, that is, has no use other than to offer its all to all, so that others too may be just such autonomous and happy personalities. This is a law of nature; normally man tends toward this. But there is one hair here, a very fine hair, which, if it falls into the mechanism, will at once crack and destroy everything. Namely: the misfortune to have here even the slightest calculation for one's own advantage. For example, I come and sacrifice my whole self for the sake of all; well, it is necessary that I sacrifice myself completely, once and for all, without any thought for gain, without in the least thinking that I am sacrificing my whole self to society and, for this, society will offer its whole self to me. The sacrifice must be made in just such a way as to offer all and even wish that you receive nothing in return, that no one will in any way be obligated to you. How is this to be done? After all, it is like trying not to think of a polar bear. Try to pose for yourself this task: not to think of a polar bear, and you will see that the cursed thing will come to mind every minute. So how is it to be done? There is no way it can be done, but rather *it must happen of itself; it must be present in one's nature,* unconsciously a part of the nature of the whole race, in a word: in order for there to be a principle of brotherly love there must be love. It is necessary to be drawn by one's very instincts into brotherhood, community, and harmony, to be drawn in spite of all the nation's age-old sufferings, in spite of the barbaric crudity deeply rooted in the nation, in spite of age-old slavery, in spite of foreigners—in a word, the need for a brotherly community must be in the nature of man; he must be born with it, or he must have been in the habit from time immemorial. What would brotherhood consist of if it were put into rational, conscious language? Of this: each separate individual, without any compulsion, without any benefit to himself, would say to society, "We are strong only when we are together; take everything from me, if you require that of me; do not think of me as you make your laws; do not be at all concerned about me; I offer you all my rights; dispose of me as you please. This is my highest happiness: to sacrifice everything to you and to do you no harm in doing so. I shall annihilate myself, I shall melt away with complete indifference, if only your brotherhood will flourish and endure." The brotherhood, on the other hand, must say, "You offer us too much. We have no right not to accept what you offer us, for you yourself say that in this lies all your happiness; but what is to be done, when in our hearts we are constantly concerned about your happiness? Take everything that is ours too. Every minute and with all our strength we shall try to increase your personal freedom and self-revelation as much as possible. Do not fear any enemies now, either among people or in nature. We are all behind you; we all guarantee your safety; we are forever doing our utmost for you because we are brothers; we are all your brothers; there are many of us, and we are strong: so be at peace and of good cheer, fear nothing, and rely on us."

Needless to say, after this there is nothing to divide up, since here everything will be shared of itself. Love one another, and all these things will be added unto you.

Now there is Utopia indeed, gentlemen! Everything is grounded in feeling, in nature, not in reason. To be sure, this is even a kind of humiliation of reason. What do you think? Is it a Utopia or not?

But, again, what is the socialist to do if there is no basis for brotherhood in Western man but, on the contrary, an individualist, isolationist foundation that continually gives itself a bad name and demands its rights with a sword in its hand? Seeing that there is no brotherhood, the socialist begins to urge brotherhood. In the absence of brotherhood, he wants to create, to shape brotherhood. In order to make rabbit stew, one must first of all have a rabbit. But there is no rabbit, that is, no nature capable of brotherhood, no nature that believes in brotherhood, no nature that is drawn to brotherhood on its own. In despair the socialist begins to act, to define a future brotherhood; he calculates the weight and the measure, entices people with the advantages, explains, teaches, and recounts who will receive how much from this brotherhood, what each will win; he determines what each individual will look like and the burden allotted to each, determines in advance an accounting of earthly blessings; who will earn how much of them and what each must voluntarily turn over to society in exchange, to the detriment of his individuality. But what kind of brotherhood will it be if they divide and determine in advance who has earned how much and what each one must do? However, the formula "one for all and all for one" has been proclaimed. Nothing better than this, of course, could be thought of, especially since the whole formula was taken from one of those books known to us all. But they began to apply this formula to the cause, and six months later the brothers dragged Cabet,[4] the founder of the brotherhood, into court. It is said that the Fourierists[5] have taken the last 900,000 francs of their capital and are still struggling to somehow establish a brotherhood. Nothing is coming of it. Of course, there is a great attraction in living, if not on a brotherly basis, then on a purely rational basis, that is, in living well, when they guarantee everything and demand only your labor and your consent. But here once again, an enigma enters in: it seems that they indeed offer the man a guarantee, promise to feed him and give him drink and to provide him with work, and for this they demand of him only a little drop of his personal freedom for the sake of the general welfare, a very, very little drop. But no, a man does not want to live even according to these calculations, for even a little drop is hard for him to give up. In his foolishness it seems to him that this is a prison and that he is better off all by himself, because that way he is free. And in his freedom, you know, he is beaten, he is offered no work, he dies of hunger, and he has no freedom at all; and yet it seems to this odd fellow that he is better off with his freedom. Needless to say, the socialist can only spit and tell him he is a fool, an immature adolescent who does not understand what is good for him; that an ant, a dumb, insignificant ant, is more intelligent than he because in the anthill everything runs so well, everything is so regulated, all are well-fed and happy, each knows his business, in a word: man is still a long way from the anthill.

In other words, socialism is quite possible, but only in places other than France.

And so at the height of his despair the socialist finally proclaims, "*Liberté, égalité, fraternité où la mort.*" Well, here there is nothing left to say, and the bourgeois triumphs once and for all.

And if the bourgeois triumphs, then the formula of Sieyès is realized, literally and to the last detail. Since the bourgeois is everything, why is he embarrassed, why is he all huddled up, what is he afraid of? All the others have made fools of themselves, all have proven bankrupt before him. Formerly, in the time of Louis-Philippe for instance, the bourgeois was never so embarrassed or afraid, and yet he reigned then too. Yes, but then he was still struggling; he sensed that he had enemies and settled accounts with them for the last time with rifle and bayonet on the June barricades.[6] But the battle ended, and the bourgeois saw that he was alone on earth, that there was nothing better than he, that he was the ideal, that it was no longer left to him, as it was before, to convince the world that he is the ideal but simply to pose calmly and majestically for the entire world as the image of ultimate beauty and the greatest possible human perfection. The position is, if you will, embarrassing. Napoleon III came to the rescue. He fell to them as though from the sky, as the one way out of the difficulty, as the one possibility remaining at the time. Since that very moment the bourgeois has prospered, has paid a terrible price for his prosperity, and fears everything precisely because he has attained everything. When you have attained everything, it becomes painful to lose *everything*. And from this, my friends, it directly follows that he who fears most is the one who prospers most. Please do not laugh. Isn't that the way it is with the bourgeois of today?

7

A Continuation of
the Foregoing

And why are there *so many flunkeys among the bourgeoisie,*
especially those with such a noble appearance? Please do not
accuse me, do not cry out that I am exaggerating, slandering,
that the hatred in me is speaking. Hatred toward what? Toward whom? Why hatred? There are simply many flunkeys,
and that is all there is to it. Cringing servility is eating its way
more and more into the bourgeois nature, and more and more
it is considered a virtue. And that is how it must be in the
present order of things. It is a natural outcome. But the main
point, the main point is that this very nature helps it along.
I am not saying that there is a strong innate tendency toward
spying, for example, in the bourgeois. My opinion is just that
the extraordinary development of spying in France—and not
simple but masterly spying, spying as a calling, developed to
the point of an art, with its own scientific methods—is the
result of their inborn servility. What ideally noble Gustave
who still does not have enough things will not hand over the
letters of his loved one for ten thousand francs or betray his
lover to her husband? I may be exaggerating, but perhaps what
I say is based on certain facts. The Frenchman passionately
loves to get ahead, to look good in the eyes of those in power
and cringe before them, even quite disinterestedly, even without expecting any reward at the moment, on credit, for the
ledger. Recall, for example, all those seeking positions during

the frequent changes in the government that took place in France. Recall the pranks and the tricks they pulled and what they themselves admitted. Recall one of the *Iambes* of Barbier[1] on this subject. One day in a cafe I picked up a certain newspaper dated 3 July. I take a look: letters from Vichy. The Emperor was visiting Vichy at the time, with his court, of course; there were cavalcades and festivities. The correspondent describes it all. He begins:

"We have many excellent horsemen. No doubt you have already guessed who is the most brilliant of them all. His Majesty rides every day in the company of his suite" and so on.

It is understandable that one might be carried away by the brilliant qualities of one's emperor. One may revere his mind, his prudence, his perfections, and so on. And you must not say to such a reverent gentleman's face that he is dissembling. "It is my conviction, and that is the end of it," he will answer you, which is exactly how some of our own modern journalists would answer you. Understand: he is secure; he has an answer for you that will shut your mouth. The freedom of conscience and convictions is the first and foremost freedom in the world. But in this case, what can he answer you? Here, you know, he is not looking at the laws of reality; he is trampling down all credibility and is doing so intentionally. And what reason might there be for doing this intentionally? After all, no one will believe him. The horseman himself probably will not read it, and even if he does, it is possible that the Frenchman who wrote the "correspondence," the newspaper that featured it, and the paper's editorial staff are all so stupid that they do not realize that the sovereign has absolutely no need for the glory of being the premiere horseman in France, that at his age he gives absolutely no thought to this glory, and that he will not believe he is the most skillful horseman in all of France, even if they assure him that he is; it is said that he is an extremely intelligent man. No, something else is at work here: let it be implausible and ridiculous, let the sovereign himself look upon it with disgust and disdainful laughter, let him, let him; he will see the blind submission, the boundless adulation, slavish, stupid, implausible, but nonetheless *adulation,* and that is the main thing. Now consider: if this were not in the spirit of the nation; if such base flattery were not considered completely possible, ordinary, completely within the order of things, and even proper, then would it be possible to place such a report in a Paris newspaper? Where do you find flattery of this kind in print, except in France? I speak of the spirit of the nation precisely because not just one newspaper carries on this way, but almost all of them are of just this type, with the exception of two or three that are not completely dependent.

I was once sitting at a table d'hôte, not in France but in Italy, although there were many Frenchmen at the table. They were talking about Garibaldi. At that time everyone was talking about Garibaldi. It was about two weeks before Aspromonte.[2] Needless to say, they were talking very mysteriously; some remained silent and did not want to express their opinions at all; others shook their heads. The general sense of the conversation was that Garibaldi had undertaken a risky, even an unreasonable business; but, of course, they expressed this opinion with reservations, for Garibaldi is a man on a level so far above everyone else that it might be reasonable for him to set out in a manner which, according to ordinary considerations, would be too risky. They gradually shifted over to Garibaldi's personality. They began to enumerate his qualities. The verdict was rather favorable for the Italian hero.

"No, I am surprised at only one thing about him," one Frenchman loudly declared; he had a pleasant and impressive appearance, about thirty years old, his face bearing the imprint of that unusual nobility which in all Frenchmen is striking to the point of impudence. "Only one circumstance about him surprises me very much!"

Naturally, everyone turned toward the orator with curiosity.

The new quality discovered in Garibaldi would surely be of interest to everyone.

"In 1860 he enjoyed unlimited and completely uncontrolled power for a time in Naples. He had a sum of twenty million in treasury funds at his disposal! He was accountable to no one for this sum! He could take and hide as much as he wanted from that sum, and no one would ask him anything about it! He hid away nothing and gave the government a complete accounting for the money, down to the last sou. It is almost unbelievable!"

Even his own eyes were aflame as he spoke of the twenty million francs.

You can say anything you like, of course, about Garibaldi. But to bring up the name of Garibaldi in connection with the embezzlement of treasury funds—that, of course, only a Frenchman could do.

And how naively, how candidly he spoke of it. For candor, of course, everything is forgiven, even the loss of the ability to understand and to have a flair for genuine honor; but having

looked into that face so played out at the recollection of the
twenty million, I happened to think, "And what if you, brother,
instead of Garibaldi, had found yourself with the state treasury at that time?"

You will tell me that, again, this is wrong, that it is merely
an isolated incident, that exactly the same thing happens among
us, and that I cannot vouch for all Frenchmen. This is true, of
course, and I am not talking about all of them. There is ineffable nobility everywhere, and among us it has perhaps even
been much worse. But why hold it up as a virtue, mind you?
Do you know what? It is possible even for a scoundrel not to
lose his flair for honor; but here, you see, there are many honorable people, yet they have completely lost their flair for honor
and thus act in a base manner for the sake of virtue without
realizing what they are doing. The former, certainly, is more
depraved, but the latter, if you will, is more contemptible. Such
a catechism on virtue points up a bad symptom in the life of
a nation. I do not want to argue the matter of isolated incidents
with you. For after all, an entire nation consists only of certain
isolated incidents, does it not?

This, in fact, is what I think. Perhaps I was mistaken about
the bourgeois's being all huddled up and about his still being
afraid of something. As for being all huddled up, he really is
all huddled up and is rather frightened, but overall the bourgeois enjoys complete prosperity. Although he indeed deceives
himself, although he declares to himself every minute that
everything is all right, this in no way disturbs his apparent
self-confidence. Further, whenever his spirits are running high,
he is terribly self-confident even on the inside. How all this can
be compatible in him is truly a puzzle, but it is so. Generally,
the bourgeois is far from stupid; however, he does not have
much in the way of brains but only fragments of a brain, as
it were. He has a frightful supply of ready-made ideas, like
firewood for the winter, and he seriously intends to live by
them for a thousand years. But what is a thousand years? The
bourgeois rarely mentions a thousand years, and then only
when he slips into eloquence. "*Aprés moi le déluge*" is far more
common and is more often applied to the matter at hand. And
what indifference to everything, what transient, empty interests. In Paris I used to go to a place where a large number of
people occupied my time. It was as though they were all afraid
to speak of anything out of the ordinary, anything that was
not trivial, anything of general interest; well, in that place
there was nothing of general interest. I do not think there

could be any fear of spies here; it is simply that they have all forgotten how to think and speak about anything more serious. Here, however, I met people who were terribly interested in the impression Paris had made on me, how much reverence I had for it, how amazed, overwhelmed, and annihilated I was. The Frenchman still thinks that he is capable of being morally overwhelming and annihilating. This too is a rather amusing sign. I especially remember one very nice, very amiable, very kind old gentleman whom I sincerely liked. He would look me in the eye, asking for my opinion of Paris, and was terribly grieved when I did not express any particular delight. There was even a look of suffering on his kind face, literally suffering—I am not exaggerating. Oh, dear Monsieur Le M—re! You will never dissuade the Frenchman, that is, the Parisian (because, you see, in essence all Frenchmen are Parisians), from his belief that he is the foremost man on the face of the earth. Except for Paris, however, he knows very little about the face of the earth. Indeed, he really does not want to know. This is a national trait, even the most characteristic one. But the most characteristic trait of the Frenchman is eloquence. His love for eloquence is inextinguishable and burns brighter and brighter as the years go by. I would really like to find out just when this love for eloquence began in France. The major part of it, certainly, began under Louis XIV. It is remarkable that in France everything began under Louis XIV; it is true. But the most remarkable thing of all is that everything in Europe began under Louis XIV. Why this king was so successful, I cannot understand! After all, he is not particularly greater than all the earlier kings. Perhaps it is because he was the first to say, "*L'état c'est moi.*" This delighted everyone enormously; it spread all over Europe at the time. I think this utterance alone made him famous. Louis XIV was a most nationalistic sovereign, completely in the French spirit, so that I absolutely do not understand how all those little pranks could have taken place in France . . . well, at the end of the last century, I mean. They played their pranks and then returned to the former spirit; and so it goes; but eloquence, eloquence, oh, that is a stumbling block for the Parisian. He is ready to forget everything from earlier times, everything, everything, ready to carry on the most sensible conversations and to be the most obedient and diligent child, but eloquence and eloquence alone he still cannot forget. He pines and sighs for eloquence; he recalls Theirs, Guizot, Odilon, Barrot.[3] "There was such eloquence then," he sometimes says to himself and gets lost in reverie. Napoleon III understood this and immediately resolved that Jacques Bon-homme should not daydream, and he gradually introduced el-oquence. For this purpose, six liberal deputies are kept in the legislative body, six permanent, immutable, genuine liberal deputies, that is, such as you perhaps could not bribe even if you tried, and, for all that, there are nonetheless only six—six there were, six there are, and just six will remain. No more will get in, don't worry; but there will not be any fewer either. And at first glance, this is a very clever trick. The whole mat-ter, however, is much simpler in reality and is managed with the help of *sufferage universel*. Needless to say, all the appro-priate measures are taken in order to keep them from talking too much. But chatting is allowed. Every year at the appointed time the most important questions of state are discussed, and the Parisian is in a state of sweet excitement. He knows that there will be eloquence, and he is glad. Of course, he knows very well that there will be only eloquence and nothing more, that there will be words, words, words, and that decidedly noth-ing will result from these words. But he is very, very satisfied even with this. And he is the first to find all this extremely sensible. The speeches of some of these six representatives enjoy a special popularity. And the representative is always prepared to give a speech for the amusement of the public. It is a strange affair: you see, even he is completely certain that nothing will come of his speech, that it is all just a farce and nothing more, an innocent game, a masquerade, and yet he speaks, for several years on end he speaks and speaks beau-tifully, even with great pleasure. And the mouths of the mem-bers who listen to him water with pleasure. "The man speaks well!" And the President's mouth waters, as does every mouth in France. But once the representative has finished, the tutor of these nice, well-behaved children stands up. He solemnly announces that the essay on the assigned topic "The Rising of the Sun" was excellently approached and developed by the hon-orable orator. "We are amazed at the talent of the honorable orator," he says, "at his thoughts and at the good conduct ex-pressed in those thoughts; we were delighted, all of us, all. . . . But although the honorable member has fully earned as a re-ward a book with the inscription 'For good conduct and success in the sciences,' in spite of that, gentlemen, the honorable representative's speech, viewed from higher considerations, is not fit for anything. I hope, gentlemen, that you will agree with me entirely." At this point he turns to all the represen-tatives, and his eyes are glaring with severity. The representatives whose mouths had been watering immediately applaud their tutor with frantic enthusiasm and at the same time congratulate and movingly shake the representative's hand for the pleasure provided; they ask him to provide them with this liberal pleasure next time, with the tutor's permission. The tutor benevolently grants permission; the author of the account of "The Rising of the Sun" withdraws, proud of his success; the representatives withdraw, licking their lips, to the bosom of their families, and in the evening they joyfully stroll arm in arm with their spouses at the Palais Royal, listening to the babbling spouts of the beneficent little fountains; and the tutor, having reported everything to the proper authorities, announces to all of France that everything is all right.

Sometimes, however, when matters become somewhat more important, the game too gets to be somewhat more important. Prince Napoleon himself is brought to one of the meetings. Prince Napoleon suddenly begins to take up the opposition, to the utter fright of all the young pupils. There is a solemn silence in the classroom. Prince Napoleon plays the liberal; the Prince does not agree with the government; in a word, he says exactly what (it is assumed) these nice children might have said if the tutor were to leave the classroom for a moment. Of course, even then it would be within limits; indeed, the assumption is absurd because all these nice children have been so nicely educated that they would not so much as stir even if the tutor were to be away from them for a whole week. And so when Prince Napoleon finishes, the tutor stands up and solemnly announces that the essay on the assigned topic "The Rising of the Sun" was excellently approached and developed by the honorable orator. "We were amazed at the talent, at the eloquent thoughts and the good conduct of the All Merciful Prince. . . . We are ready to present him with a book for his diligence and success in the sciences, but . . ." and so on, that is, everything that was said before; needless to say, the entire class applauds with delight, to the point of frenzy; the Prince is driven home; the well-behaved pupils file out of the classroom like good little boys, and in the evening they stroll with their spouses at the Palais Royal, listening to the babbling spouts of the beneficent little fountains, and so on, and so on, and so on; in a word, it is amazing how order is maintained.

We once lost our way in *la salle de Pas Perdue,** and instead

---

*The Hall of the Lost Way.

of the section where criminal cases are tried, we wound up in the section for civil cases. A curly-haired lawyer in cap and gown gave a speech and spouted pearls of eloquence. The president, judges, lawyers, and listeners were swimming in delight. There was a most reverent silence; we walked in on tiptoe. The matter concerned an inheritance; some hermit priests were involved in it. Hermit priests are forever involved in cases now, mainly those concerning inheritances. The most scandalous, the most vile incidents are brought to light; but the public remains silent and is hardly scandalized because the hermit priests now have substantial power, and the bourgeois is extremely well behaved. More and more the priests abide by the view that a little capital is the best thing, better than these dreams and such, and that if you save a little money, then you may have some power; and what good is eloquence? Eloquence alone is not enough now. But, as I see it, they are somewhat mistaken in this last instance. Certainly, a little capital is a wonderful thing, but with eloquence one can do a great deal with a Frenchman. The wives especially succumb to the hermit priests even more now than was dreamed of before. There is a hope that the bourgeois too will take this turn. In the trial it came out as to how the hermits, through years of cunning, even scientific pressure (they have made a science of this), burdened the soul of a beautiful and very wealthy lady; how they enticed her to come to live with them in the monastery; how there they intimidated her with various fears to the point of illness, to the point of hysterics, all in a calculated manner, with scientific gradualness. How, finally, they did make her ill, to the point of idiocy, and professed to her, finally, that to see her relatives was a great sin before the Lord God, and little by little they isolated her completely from her relatives. "Even her niece—that virginal, childlike soul, a fifteen-year-old angel of purity and innocence—even she did not dare to enter the cell of the aunt she adored, who loved her more than anything in the world and who, as the result of insidious schemes, could not even embrace her and kiss her *front virginal,*[*] where the white angel of innocence was enthroned. . . ." In a word, the whole thing went like that; it was remarkably good. The lawyer who spoke himself seemed to melt with the joy of knowing how to speak well; the president melted; the public melted. The hermit priests lost the battle solely as the result of eloquence.

---

[*] Virginal forehead.

Of course, they did not lose heart. They lost one; they will win fifteen.

"Who is that lawyer?" I asked one young student who was among the reverent listeners. Many students were there, and all of them were so very well behaved. He looked at me in amazement.

"Jules Favre!" he finally answered with such disdainful vexation that I could not but feel ashamed. Thus I had the occasion to become acquainted with the flower of French eloquence, so to speak, at its primary source.

But there is an infinitude of these sources. The bourgeois is eaten to the very bone with eloquence. We once went into the Panthéon to have a look at the great men. It was an inopportune time, and they asked us for two francs. Then a decrepit and venerable invalid took the keys and led us into the church vaults. He spoke like a human being all along the way, though he mumbled a little due to his missing teeth. But upon reaching the vaults, he slowly began to sing as he led us up to the first tomb.

"*Ci-gît Voltaire*—Voltaire, that great genius of our magnificent France. He uprooted prejudices, destroyed ignorance, struggled against the angel of darkness, and wielded the torch of enlightenment. In his tragedies he achieved greatness, although France already had a Corneille."

He was obviously speaking from something he had memorized. Someone had once written the oration for him on a sheet of paper, and he had learned it by heart for the rest of his life; the pleasure began to shine on his old, good-natured face as he started spreading his high-flown word.

"*Ci-gît Jean-Jacques Rousseau*," he continued, walking up to the next tomb. "*Jean-Jacques, l'homme de la nature et de vérité!*"[4]

It suddenly struck me as funny. The high-flown word debases everything. Indeed, it was apparent that the poor old man, speaking of *nature* and *vérité,* had no idea of what he was talking about.

"Strange!" I said to him. "Of these two great men, one spent his whole life calling the other a liar and an evil man, while the other would call the first a simple fool. And yet here they have ended up almost one next to the other."

"Monsieur, monsieur!" the invalid put in, wishing to object, but, nonetheless, he did not object and quickly led us to the next tomb.

"*Ci-gît Lannes,* Marshal Lannes," he sang out again, "one

of the greatest heroes France has ever had, as abundant as she is in her heroes. Not only was he a great marshal and the most highly skilled leader of troops, with the exception of the great Emperor, but he enjoyed a still greater well-being. He was a friend . . ."[5]

"Well, yes, he was a friend of Napoleon," I said, wanting to cut the speech short.

"Monsieur! Allow me to speak!" the old pensioner interrupted me; his voice sounded as though he were slightly hurt.

"Speak, speak, I am listening."

"But he enjoyed a still greater well-being. He was a friend of the great Emperor. Not one of all his other marshals had the good fortune of becoming a friend of the great man. Only Marshal Lannes was awarded this great honor. When he lay dying for his fatherland on the field of battle . . ."

"Well, yes, both of his legs were torn off by a shell."

"Monsieur, monsieur! Allow me to say it myself!" the invalid cried in an almost mournful voice. "Perhaps you know all this . . . but allow me to tell it!"

The odd fellow wanted terribly to tell it himself, even though we already knew all about it.

"When he lay dying," he picked up again, "for his fatherland on the field of battle, the Emperor, stricken to the heart and bemoaning the great loss . . ."

"Came to bid him farewell," something possessed me to interrupt him again, and I immediately felt that I had done wrong; I was even ashamed of myself.

"Monsieur, monsieur!" the old man said, looking into my eyes with mournful reproach and shaking his gray head. "Monsieur! I know, I am certain, that you know all this, perhaps better than I. But, after all, you yourself hired me to show you: allow me to tell it myself. There is not much left now. . . .

"Then the Emperor, stricken to the heart and bemoaning (alas! to no end) the great loss which he, the Army, and all of France had suffered, drew near to the deathbed and with his last farewell alleviated the cruel sufferings of the commander who was dying before his very eyes."

"*C'est fini, monsieur,*" he added, reproachfully looking at me, and then he walked on.

"Here too is a tomb; well, they are . . . *quelques sénateurs,*"* he added indifferently, carelessly nodding his head toward sev-

---

*Some senators.

eral other tombs situated nearby. All of his eloquence had been spent on Voltaire, Jean-Jacques, and Marshal Lannes. This was truly a first-hand example, so to speak, of the people's love for eloquence. Can it be that all those orators' speeches in the National Assembly, the Convention, and the clubs, in which the people take part almost directly and through which they have been reeducated, have left a trace of only one thing in them—a love of eloquence for the sake of eloquence?

8

Bribri and Ma Biche

And what about the spouses? The spouses are in clover, as I have already said. Incidentally, why, you will ask, do I write *spouses* instead of *wives*? The high-flown word, gentlemen, that is why. When he starts to speak in a high-flown manner, the bourgeois always says *mon épouse*. And although in other strata of society, like everywhere else, they simply say *ma femme*—my wife—it is better to follow the national spirit of the majority and of high-flown expression. It is more characteristic. There are other appelations too. Whenever the bourgeois is deeply moved or wants to deceive his wife, he always calls her *ma biche.** And, conversely, the loving wife in fits of graceful playfulness calls her sweet bourgeois *bribri,†* which, for his part, is very satisfying to the bourgeois. *Bribri* and *ma biche* prosper all the time, more now than ever before. Besides the fact that it has been settled (and almost without any discussion) that in our troubled times *ma biche* and *bribri* ought to serve as models of virtue, concord, and the paradisiacal state of society in reproach to the vile ravings of the absurd communist vagrants—besides that, with each year *bribri* becomes more and more complaisant in his marital relations. He

---

*My little nanny goat.
†Little bird.

realizes that no matter what he says or how he arranges things *ma biche* cannot be restrained, that the Parisienne was created to have a lover, that it is almost impossible for a husband to manage without the coiffure; needless to say, he keeps quiet as long as he has a little money saved and has not acquired many things yet. But when these two conditions are fulfilled, *bribri* generally becomes more demanding because he begins to respect himself a great deal. Well, here he begins to look upon even Gustave differently, especially if the latter is a ragamuffin to boot and does not have very many things. A Parisian with a little money who wants to get married will usually choose a bride with a little money. Moreover, as a preliminary they square their accounts, and if it turns out that francs and things are the same on both sides, then they mate. It happens this way everywhere, but here the law of the equality of pockets has particularly become the custom. If, for example, the bride has a single kopek more than he, then she will not have that suitor but will look for a better *bribri*. Besides that, marriages based on love are becoming more and more impossible and are considered almost improper. This sensible custom of a mandatory equality of the pockets and the marriage of capital is very rarely violated, much more rarely here, I think, than anywhere else. The bourgeois does very well at putting the possession of his wife's money to his own benefit. That is why in many instances he is prepared to look through his fingers at the adventures of *ma biche* and to ignore other annoying things, because otherwise, that is, in case of a disagreement, the question of the dowry can be unpleasantly raised. Not only that, if *ma biche* should parade about in clothes they cannot afford, then *bribri,* though he notices all of it, reconciles himself: his wife is asking him for less money for clothes. Then his wife is much more complaisant. Finally, since marriage for the most part is marriage of capital and there is very little concern for mutual inclination, *bribri* has no problem with dropping in somewhere away from *ma biche* on the side. Thus it is best not to bother each other. That way there is more harmony in the household, and the sweet murmur of the sweet names *bribri* and *ma biche* will be heard more and more often between the spouses. And finally, if all is to be told, *bribri* has been remarkably successful in providing for himself even along these lines. The police commissioner is at his service every minute. That's how it is according to the laws which he has set up for himself. In an extreme case, upon catching the lovers *en fla-*

grant délit,* he may kill them both, you see, and have nothing to answer for. *Ma biche* knows this and speaks well of it herself. Through a long tutelage *ma biche* has been brought to the point where, unlike women in other barbaric and ridiculous lands, she neither grumbles nor dreams of studying in universities, for example, or of taking part in clubs or being deputies. She would rather remain in her present aerial and, so to speak, canarylike position. She is dressed up, adorned with gloves, taken to festivals; she dances and munches candy; outwardly she is received like a czarina, and the man grovels before her in the dust. This form of relationships has been worked out with surprising success and propriety. In a word, chivalrous relationships are observed, and what more could she desire? After all, they will not take Gustave away from her. Nor does she need any virtuous, lofty goal in life, and so on, and so on; in essence, she is every bit as much a capitalist and mercenary as her spouse. When the canary years have passed, that is, when she reaches the point where there is no way she can deceive herself any longer and consider herself a canary; when the possibility of a new Gustave becomes a decided absurdity, even for the most ardent and proud imagination, then suddenly *ma biche* is quickly and pitifully regenerated. All the coquetry, finery, and playfulness disappear For the most part, she becomes malicious and domineering. She attends church and accumulates money with her husband, and a certain cynicism will suddenly creep in at every turn: suddenly weariness, vexation, crude instincts, an aimlessness of existence, and cynical conversation appear. Some of them even become slovenly. Of course, they are not all this way; of course, there are other, brighter phenomena; of course, there are such social relationships everywhere, but . . . here it is all more in its own element, more original, more distinctive, more complete; here it is all more national. Here is the wellspring and embryo of that bourgeois social form which now reigns all over the world as an eternal imitation of a great nation.

Yes, outwardly *ma biche* is a czarina. It is difficult even to imagine the specified politeness, the importunate attention, that surrounds her everywhere in society and on the street. The subtlety is amazing; it sometimes reaches the point of such Manilovism[1] that an honest soul would find it unbearable. The blatant falseness of the counterfeit would insult him to

---

*At the scene of the crime.

the depths of his heart. But *ma biche* herself is a great swin-
dler, and . . . that is all she needs. . . . She always gets her way
and always prefers to cheat rather than walk straight and hon-
estly: it is more correct, in her opinion, and certainly more of
a game. After all, the game, the intrigue, is everything to *ma
biche;* there lies the main thing. Yet how she dresses, how she
walks down the street. *Ma biche* is affected, seasoned, completely unnatural, but this is what is so captivating, especially
for blasé and somewhat depraved people who have lost their
taste for fresh, spontaneous beauty. *Ma biche* was brought up
very badly; she has the small mind and the small heart of a
bird, but, to make up for it, she is graceful; she has innumer-
able secrets of such tricks and fancies that you are subdued
and follow her around like a savory novelty. She is even rarely
attractive. There is something malicious in her face. But that
is nothing: it is a lively face, playful, and it possesses the mystery of a counterfeit of feeling and nature to a remarkable
degree. Perhaps what you like about her is not exactly that
she attains the natural by means of the counterfeit; rather, it
is the very process of counterfeiting that fascinates you; it is
the art itself that fascinates you. For the most part, genuine
love and a good counterfeit of love are both the same to the
Parisian. He might even prefer the counterfeit. A certain Ori-
ental attitude toward women is showing up in Paris more and
more. Camille[2] is more and more in fashion. "Take my money
and utterly deceive me, that is, counterfeit your love." That is
what they demand of Camelia. They demand little more of
their spouses, or at least they are satisfied with this, and so
Gustave is tacitly and condescendingly tolerated. The bourgeois knows, moreover, that *ma biche* will share all of his interests in her old age and will be a most enthusiastic aide to
him in accumulating money. She even helps a great deal in
her youth. She sometimes runs the entire business and attracts
buyers; in a word, she is his right hand, his chief shop assis-
tant. How can she not be forgiven a Gustave or two? On the
street a woman is inviolable. No one insults her, everyone yields
to her, not the way it is among us, where a woman who is the
least bit young cannot take two steps on the street without
some military or derelict physiognomy peeking under her hat
and suggesting that they get acquainted.

Despite the possibility of a Gustave, however, the ordinary,
ritualistic form of the relations between *bribri* and *ma biche*
is rather nice and often even naive. Generally, foreigners—this
was quite striking to me—are almost all incomparably more

naive than Russians. It is difficult to explain this in more spe-
cific terms; you have to see it for yourself. *"Le Russe est scep-
tique et moqueur,"** the Frenchman say of us, and it is true. We
are more cynical; we hold what is our own less dear; we do not
even like what is our own, or at least we do not respect it to
any great degree, failing to understand what it is. We devote
ourselves to European interests and to the general interests of
humanity and belong to no nation; thus we naturally have a
cooler relationship to everything, as if out of obligation, and
in any case a more abstract relationship. However, I have di-
gressed from the subject. *Bribri* is sometimes extremely naive.
While strolling around the fountains, for example, he will start
to explain to *ma biche* why the fountains spurt upward; he
explains the laws of nature to her; he expresses to her a nationalistic pride in the beauty of the Boulogne woods, the lighting, the play of *les grandes eaux* of Versailles, the victories of
the Emperor Napoleon, and *gloire militaire;* he takes delight
in her curiosity and her pleasure and is quite satisfied with it
all. Even the most roguish *ma biche* treats her spouse rather
tenderly, that is, not with any sort of counterfeit tenderness
but with an unselfish tenderness, despite the spouse's coiffure.
Of course, I do not pretend to lift the roofs from the houses,
like Le Sage's[3] devil. I relate only what has struck me, only
the way it seems to me. *"Mon mari n'a pas encore vu la mer,"†*
another *ma biche* says to you, and there is a sincere, naive
condolence in her voice. This means that her husband still has
not gone to Brest or Boulogne to look at the sea. It must be
known that the bourgeois has certain highly naive and highly
serious needs which have almost been transformed into general
bourgeois habits. Besides the need to hoard and the need for
eloquence, the bourgeois, for example, has two more needs, two
of the most legitimate needs sanctified by universal habit and
which he treats extremely seriously, almost pathetically. The
first need is *voir la mer,* to see the sea. The Parisian sometimes
spends his whole life doing business in Paris and never sees
the sea. Why does he need to see the sea? He himself does not
know, but has an intense, passionate desire; he postpones the
trip year after year because his business usually detains him;
he grieves, and his wife sincerely shares his grief. There is
usually much that is genuinely felt here, and I respect it. He

---

*"The Russian is a skeptic and a mocker."
†"My husband has not seen the sea yet."

finally succeeds in finding the time and the means; he packs
his bags and goes to "see the sea" for a few days. When he
returns, he pompously and enthusiastically tells his wife, his
relatives, and his friends about his impressions, and for the
rest of his life he has sweet memories of how he saw the sea.
The other legitimate and no less powerful need of the bourgeois, and especially the Parisian bourgeois, is *se rouler dans
l'herbe.** The point is that once the Parisian leaves town he
exceedingly loves and even considers it a duty to roll in the
grass; he even fulfills this need with dignity, feeling that in
doing so he joins himself *avec la nature,* and he particularly
loves it if someone is watching him at the time. Generally,
when the Parisian is out of town, he at once considers it to be
his duty to immediately become more free and easy, more playful, even more dashing, in a word, to look more natural, a man
closer to *la nature. L'homme de la nature et de la vérité!* Isn't
it since Jean-Jacques that the bourgeois has had this urgent
respect for *la nature?* For the most part, however, the Parisian
permits himself both of these needs—*voir la mer* and *se rouler
dans l'herbe*—only when he has achieved status for himself, in
a word, only when he is beginning to respect himself, is proud
of himself, and looks upon himself as a human being. *Se rouler
dans l'herbe* is even twice, ten times as sweet when it happens
on his own land, purchased with money that he has earned by
his labor. When he retires from business, the bourgeois generally likes to buy some land somewhere and acquire a home,
a garden, a fence, chickens, a cow. It does not matter if it is all
on the most microscopic scale—the bourgeois is filled with the
most childlike, the most touching delight. *"Mon arbre, mon
mur,"†* he says over and over to himself and to everyone who
calls on him, and he will not stop repeating it every minute for
the rest of his life. Here it is sweetest of all *se rouler dans
l'herbe.* In order to fulfill this obligation, he does not fail to put
in a lawn for himself in front of his house. Someone was telling
me that one bourgeois could not get a bit of grass to grow in
the area designated for his lawn. He cultivated, irrigated, and
transplanted grass from other spots, but nothing would come
up or take in the sand. Then, it seems, he bought himself an
artificial lawn; he made a special trip to Paris for it, ordered
himself a circular grass carpet one sagene in diameter, and

---

*To roll in the grass.
†"My tree, my wall."

spread out the rug of long grass every afternoon just to fool himself and satisfy his legitimate need to roll around in the grass. The bourgeois is quite capable of this in the first moments of ecstasy over his acquisition of property, so there is nothing morally implausible here.

But a couple of words about Gustave too. Gustave, of course, is the same as the bourgeois, that is, a salesman, merchant, functionary, *homme de lettres,* officer. Gustave is not married, but he is the same *bribri.* But that is not the point; rather, it is a matter of how Gustave dresses and drapes himself these days, what he looks like, what sort of feathers he wears. The ideal of Gustave changes with the times and is always reflected in the theatre according to the form that prevails in society. The bourgeois has a special liking for vaudeville, but he likes melodrama even more. Modest and merry vaudeville is the one work of art which cannot be transplanted to any other soil but is able to live only in the place of its birth, in Paris. Although vaudeville fascinates the bourgeois, it does not completely satisfy him. The bourgeois considers it trivial. He needs the lofty, he needs ineffable nobility, he needs sensitivity, and melodrama contains all of this. Melodrama will never die as long as the bourgeois is alive. It is curious that now even vaudeville is being regenerated. It is still just as merry and outrageously funny as ever, but now another element is beginning to be mixed with it in a powerful way—moral preaching. The bourgeois very much loves and now regards it as a sacred and necessary matter to lecture himself and *ma biche* with admonitions at every opportunity. The bourgeois, moreover, now wields unlimited power; he is power, and the mean little authors of vaudeville and melodrama are always flunkeys and always flatter power. That is why the bourgeois now triumphs even when presented in a ridiculous form, and in the end it is always announced to him that everything is all right. You have to think that such reports seriously put the bourgeois's mind at rest. Every cowardly man who is not completely convinced of the success of his affairs has an agonizing need to reassure himself, to hearten himself, to have his mind put at rest. He even begins to believe in favorable omens. That is just the way it is here. Lofty traits and lofty lessons are presented in melodrama. There is no humor here; rather, there is the pathetic triumph of all that *bribri* loves, of all that pleases him. What pleases him most of all is political tranquility and the right to accumulate money for himself for the purpose of building a more tranquil refuge. And melodramas are now characteristically written in this way. This is also characteristic of Gustave. From the portrayal of Gustave it is always possible to verify what *bribri* considers the ideal of ineffable nobility at any given moment. Formerly, long ago, Gustave was a poet, an artist, or an unrecognized genius, downtrodden, tormented by persecutions and injustices. He would fight admirably, and it always ended in such a way that the viscountess, who secretly pined over him but toward whom he was disdainfully indifferent, united him with her ward Cecilia, who did not have a kopek but who suddenly finds herself with countless millions. Gustave usually rebelled and refused the money. But at that point the exhibition of his work was crowned with success. Three ridiculous milords immediately burst into his apartment and offer him a hundred thousand francs for his next painting. Gustave disdainfully laughs at them and in bitter despair announces that all men are scoundrels unworthy of his brush, that he will not deliver up art, sacred art, to profanation by the pygmies who until now have taken no note of how great he is. But the viscountess bursts in and announces that Cecilia is dying of love for him and that therefore he must carry on with his painting. At this point Gustave guesses that the viscountess, once his enemy and because of whom not one of his paintings had yet been exhibited, secretly loves him, that she had taken revenge on him out of jealousy. It goes without saying that Gustave immediately takes the money from the three milords, cursing them once more, which leaves them quite satisfied; then he runs to Cecilia, agrees to accept her million, and forgives the viscountess, who retires to her estate; having joined in lawful wedlock, he begins to acquire children, a flannel sweater, and a *bonnet de coton** and strolls with *ma biche* in the evenings by the beneficent little fountains, the quiet babbling of their spouts reminding him, of course, of the constancy, solidity, and quietude of his earthly happiness.

Sometimes it happens that Gustave is not a salesman but some worn-out, forgotten orphan whose soul is filled with the most ineffable nobility. It suddenly turns out that he is not an orphan at all but the lawful son of Rothschild. The millions appear. But Gustave proudly and disdainfully refuses the millions. Why? It is necessary for the sake of eloquence. At this point in bursts Madame Beaupré, the banker's wife who is in love with him and whose husband employs him. She announces

---

*Nightcap.

that Cecilia is now dying from love for him and that he must go to save her. Gustave guesses that Madame Beaupré is in love with him, picks up the millions, and, cursing everyone with the most vile words because nowhere in the entire human race is there as much ineffable nobility as in himself, he goes to Cecilia and unites with her. The banker's wife goes off to her estate. Beaupré celebrates, for his wife, who had been at the edge of the precipice, still remains pure and chaste; Gustave acquires children and in the evenings goes for strolls around the beneficent little fountains, whose babbling spouts remind him and so on, and so on.

Today ineffable nobility is most often portrayed in a military officer or a military engineer or something of the kind, but most often in a military man who, without fail, has a ribbon of the Legion of Honor "purchased with his blood." Incidentally, this ribbon is terrible. Its wearer boasts about it so much that it is almost impossible to be with him, to travel with him in a train car, to sit with him in a theatre, to meet him in a restaurant. He will not even spit at you; he swaggers over you in a shameless way; he puffs and pants with such swaggering that it finally begins to nauseate you; your bile over flows, and you have to send for a doctor. But the Frenchmen are very fond of this. It is also noteworthy that in the theatre today so much special attention is paid to Monsieur Beaupré, at least much more than before. Beaupré, of course, has amassed a great deal of money and has acquired very many things. He is straightforward, simple, and a little ridiculous for his bourgeois habits and for the fact that he is a husband; but he is good, honest, magnanimous, and ineffably noble in the act where he must suffer from the suspicion that *ma biche* is unfaithful to him. Nevertheless, he magnanimously decides to forgive her. Needless to say, it turns out that she is as pure as a dove, that she was just playing a little prank, that she got carried away with Gustave, and that *bribri,* overwhelming her with his magnanimity, is the most precious of all to her. Cecilia, of course, is penniless, as before, but only in the first act; it turns out later that she has a million. Gustave is proud and disdainfully noble, as always, only he swaggers more because he is a military man. The dearest thing in the world to him is his cross, purchased with blood, and *"l'épée de mon père."* He speaks constantly of his father's sword, inappropriately, everywhere; you even fail to understand the point; he curses, spits, but everyone bows down to him, and the spectators weep and applaud (literally weep). Needless to say, he is penniless; that is a *sine qua non.* Madame Beaupré, of course, is in love with him, Cecilia too, but he does not suspect Cecilia's love. Cecilia groans with love throughout the five acts. Finally, it snows, or something of the sort. Cecilia wants to throw herself out the window. But under the window two shots ring out, and everyone comes running. Gustave, pale, his arm bandaged, slowly enters the scene. The ribbon purchased with blood glimmers on his frock coat. Cecilia's slanderer and seducer has been punished. Gustave finally forgets that Cecilia loves him and that it was all Madam Beaupré's doing. But Madame Beaupré is pale and frightened, and Gustave guesses that she loves him. But another shot rings out. It is Beaupré, killing himself out of despair. Madam Beaupré screams and rushes to the doors, but there is Beaupré carrying a dead fox or something of the sort. The lesson has been learned; *ma biche* will never forget him. She clings to *bribri,* who forgives everything. But suddenly Cecilia comes into a million, and Gustave once again rebels. He does not want to get married; Gustave grimaces; Gustave curses with vile words. It is absolutely necessary that Gustave curse with vile words and spit at the million; otherwise the bourgeois would never forgive him; there would not be enough ineffable nobility. Please do not think that the bourgeois has contradicted himself. Don't worry: the million will not pass by the happy couple; it is inevitably theirs and in the end always shows up as a reward for virtue. The bourgeois will not betray himself. In the end Gustave accepts Cecilia's million, and with that begin the inevitable little fountains, the nightcaps, the babbling spouts, and so forth and so forth. Thus there turns out to be a great deal of sensitivity, a bunch of ineffable nobility, a triumphant Beaupré overwhelming everyone with his marital virtues, and, the main and most important thing, a million in the form of fate, in the form of a natural law to which goes all honor, glory, worship, and so on, and so on. *Bribri* and *ma biche* exit the theatre completely satisfied, calmed, and consoled. Gustave accompanies them, and, helping someone else's *ma biche* into a cab, he quietly kisses her hand. . . . All is as it should be.

TRANSLATOR'S NOTES

1

1. Ann Ward Radcliffe (1764–1823), English author of *The Mysteries of Udolpho* and other gothic works.

2. A line from a poem by Aleksei Stepanovich Khomyzkov (1804–60), a Slavophile whose theological concept of *sobornost'* (organic collectivity), by which he understood the Church to be the unity of believers in Christ, strongly influenced Dostoevsky. This influence is particularly evident in *The Brothers Karamazov.*

3. Compare this line to the opening of *Notes from Underground:* "I am a sick man.... I am a spiteful man. I am an unpleasant man. I think my liver is diseased."

4. Vsevolod Vladimirovich Krestovski (1840–95), Russian poet and novelist, author of the antinihilistic novels *Panurge's Flock* and *Two Forces,* as well as *The Triumph of Baal.*

5. Nikolai Mikhailovich Karumzin (1766–1826), Russian writer and historian, author of the sentimental novel *Poor Liza* and the multi-volume *History of the Russian State,* which served as the principal source for Pushkin's *Boris Godunov.* The allusion to Karamzin's falling to his knees at the Rhine waterfall is taken from his *Letters of a Russian Traveler 1789–90,* the Russian version of the "sentimental journey" to Europe.

6. Jean-Maria Farina (1685–1766), inventor of *eau de cologne.*

2

1. Denis Ivanovich Fonvizin (1745–92), major eighteenth-century Russian dramatist, humanist, and translator of Voltaire; his most important work is *The Minor,* a comedy that critically examines social and moral values.

2. Vissarion Grigorievich Belinski (1811–48), major literary critic and spokesman for the Westernizers; he promoted social realism in literature and was largely responsible for the widespread approval of Dostoevsky's first novel, *Poor Folk.*

3. Pierre Joseph Proudhon (1809–65), French thinker and utopian socialist; Louis Blanc (1811–82), French political figure and socialist thinker; Alexandre Auguste Ledru-Rollin (1807–74), French attorney and leading figure of the second republic.

4. Petr Yakovlevich Chaadaev (1794–1856), Russian philosopher and critic of officialdom whose *Philosophical Letters* influenced Herzen,

Belinski, Bakunin, and others; the publication of the first of the *Philosophical Letters* resulted in his being officially declared insane.

5. Nikolai Alekseevich Nekrasov (1821–77), Russian poet whose poetry dealt with social issues; coeditor of *Sovremennik* (The Contemporary) and close associate of other social critics, including Chernyshevsky and Dobrolyubov. As far as I can determine, however, Belopyatkin does not appear in Nekrasov's poetry.

6. Emilyan Ivanovich Pugachev (c. 1741–75), son of a Cossack landowner who claimed to be the rightful Czar and led a peasant revolt against Catherine II in 1773–74. Pushkin wrote *The History of Pugachev*, in which he analyzed the Pugachev Rebellion in the light of social and political oppression. Material from *The History of Pugachev* was incorporated into Pushkin's famous *The Captain's Daughter*.

7. The narrator in Pushkin's *Tales of Belkin;* he is a simple provincial squire.

3

1. Grigory Aleksandrovich Potemkin (1739–91), Russian field marshall and statesman; a favorite of Catherine II, he carried out a policy of consolidation and of the absolutist state and organized punitive measures against Pugachev.

2. Mikhail Evgratovich Saltykov-Shchedrin (1826–89), Russian satirist, social critic, and champion of the peasants; he worked with Nekrasov on the *Sovremennik* and authored the socially critical work *The History of a City*. In his *Provincial Sketches* he satirized bureaucratic thinking and rule; the character Filoveritov ("lover of truth"), for example, is more concerned with rules and formulas than with truth when a crime is committed.

3. Gavrila Romanovich Derzhavin (1743–1816), major Russian poet whose poems were characterized by philosophical issues and social criticism. His major poems include "Ode to Felitsa," "God," and "The Waterfall." The hero referred to here is Potemkin, the hero of "The Waterfall."

4. A fictitious writer created by two poets, Aleksei Tolstoy (1817–75) and Aleksei Zhemchuzhnikov (1821–1908). Prutkov became the satirical personification of the complacent, vain bureaucrat. His plays include *Fantasia, Silk Lace,* and *The Reckless Turk*.

5. A city on the Dnieper estuary and key battle site where Potemkin distinguished himself in the Russo-Turkish War of 1787–91.

6. The foolish youngster and title character in Fonvizin's comedy *The Minor*.

7. *Subditel'nyi superflyu,* a Frenchified nonsense phrase used by Nozdrev in Gogol's *Dead Souls*.

8. A character mentioned in Fonvizin's play *The Brigadier*. Dostoevsky puns here on the name Gvozdilov ɛ .d on the Russian word *gvozd*, which means "nail."

9. A line from *Woe from Wit,* a comedy on social values by Aleksandr Sergeevich Griboedov (1795–1829).

10. A fantastic identity assigned to Chichikov, the main character in Gogol's *Dead Souls.* A man who goes around buying dead serfs, Chichikov is a pseudosophisticate who plays on the paranoia and insecurities of Russian landowners.

11. The main character in Turgenev's *Fathers and Sons.* Bazarov is a representative of the *raznochinnaya* intelligentsia, a group of radicals who not only objected to serfdom but also challenged the nobility's intellectual dominance and opposed the monarchy. While Turgenev opposed serfdom, he was not against the monarchy in principle. Thus he believed that the Bazarovs of Russia were very frightening and very dangerous. Standing for nothing and rejecting everything, Bazarov is a nihilist, a term coined by Turgenev.

12. A female nihilist in *Fathers and Sons.*

13. The idealistic hero of Griboedov's *Woe from Wit* (1824). Herzen saw in Chatsky a portrayal of revolutionary patriotism, protest against despotism, and the struggle for uniqueness in Russian culture. Other characters from *Woe from Wit* referred to here include Famusov, a highly conservative, patriarchal landowner; Repetilov, a prattler and tippler; Skalozub, representing military stupidity; Natal'ya Dmitrievna, the wife of Chatsky's close friend; Countess Khlestova, a wealthy, candid, and aristocratic old woman; and Molchalin, a secretary and the lover of his boss's daughter, whose name is a play on the word *molchanie,* "silence."

14. Roman prisoner of the Carthaginians who died a hero's death when he was executed for refusing to give up his allegiance to Rome.

5

1. Dostoevsky has in mind contemporary utopian socialist movements.

2. Baal ("owner" or "lord") was the ancient god of the Phoenicians and Canaanites, associated with paganism and the worship of objects.

6

1. The third estate is everything. A saying made famous by Emmanuel Joseph Sieyès.

2. French intervention in Mexico, which began in 1861; by June 1873, Napoleon III had made Maximillian of Austria Emperor of Mexico.

3. Emmanuel Joseph Sieyès (1748–1836), French abbe, political leader, and revolutionary who supported individual rights but wanted to keep real power in the hands of the enlightened bourgeoisie.

4. Etienne Cabet (1788–1856), French socialist prosecuted for criticizing the government; he attempted to establish utopian socialist communities, all of which failed, in the United States.

5. Followers of François Marie Fourier (1772–1837), French sociologist and social reformer who advocated a utopian society based on cooperative units known as phalanxes, in which about four hundred families of four members each would live and work.

6. The French Socialist Party was decisively defeated during the fighting of 24–26 June 1848.

7

1. Henri Auguste Barbier (1805–82), French dramatist, poet, and social critic; his collection of poems, *Lazarus,* describes the misery of the London poor and was taken from the *Iambes,* which came out immediately after the French Revolution and met with great popularity.

2. A mountain in Italy where Garibaldi was taken prisoner while advancing toward Rome on 27 August 1861.

3. All are nineteenth-century statesmen and historians; Louis Adolphe Thiers (1798–1877) was President of France from 1871 to 1873.

4. A man of nature and truth. This is an important phrase for Dostoevsky, since he believed, as stated in *The Brothers Karamazov,* that God lies not in strength but in truth.

5. Jean Lannes (1769–1809), French marshal under Napoleon.

8

1. After Manilov, a ridiculous, sentimental, lazy landowner in *Dead Souls.*

2. A reference to the courtesan and heroine of the novel *The Lady of the Camillias* or *Camille* by Alexandre Dumas, *fils* (1824–95). Three years after writing this novel, Dumas turned it into a play by the same title. Here Dostoevsky parodies this and other French plays of the mid-nineteenth century.

3. Alain Rene Le Sage (1668–1747), French dramatist and novelist whose picaresque novel *Gil Blas* had a strong influence on Russian and European literature.